On the Road with Joseph Smith

An Author's Diary

On the Road with Joseph Smith

An Author's Diary

by Richard Lyman Bushman

GREG KOFFORD BOOKS
SALT LAKE CITY 2007

2011 10 09 08 07   5 4 3 2 1

This volume was originally published by Mormon Artists Group as a limited
edition work in November 2006, designed by Glen Nelson. Its presentation
was a stack of unbound sheets wrapped in mouldmade paper and inserted into
a handmade cherry wood slipcase.

Greg Kofford Books, Inc.   Mormon Artists Group Press
P.O. Box 1362   Glen Nelson, director
Draper, UT 84020   457 West 57th Street #601
                                              New York, NY 10019

www.koffordbooks.com   www.mormonartistsgroup.com

Library of Congress Cataloging-in-Publication Data

Bushman, Richard L.
  On the road with Joseph Smith : an author's diary / by Richard Lyman
Bushman.
       p. cm.
  Originally published: Mormon Artists Group, 2006.
  ISBN-13: 978-1-58958-102-9
  1. Bushman, Richard L. Joseph Smith. 2. Authors--Diaries. 3. Smith,
Joseph, 1805-1844. 4. Mormons--United States--Biography. I. Title.
  BX8695.S6B876 2007
  289.3092--dc22
  [B]
                                      2007014135

Contents

Introduction

Looking back now, the publication of *Joseph Smith: Rough Stone Rolling* in 2005 all seems disconcertingly like a life plan. If my memory does not fail me, I thought about a Joseph Smith biography while still in graduate school at Harvard almost fifty years ago. In those beginning years, I was uncertain about how to justify my study of history. What was history good for? Walking home to our apartment in Shaler Lane after an evening at the Widener Library, I would devise arguments to use on my Mormon friends in the Harvard Business School, many of them skeptical about the uses of history. I did not waver in my decision to study history; I was looking for a justification of my choice. I believe it was in this time of reflection that I considered writing a biography of Joseph Smith. Work on the Prophet would give a point to my career as a historian. I wanted to contribute to the Kingdom, and studying Joseph Smith's times during my early years and then writing a biography later in life seemed like a worthy plan.

From then on, however, the idea of writing about Joseph Smith receded into the background. For years Mormon history was no more than a sideline to my primary professional interests. When I began to teach, I was hired as an early American historian based on my first book *From Puritan to Yankee: Character and the Social Order in Connecticut, 1690-1765*. I did not engage Mormon history until the 1970s when Leonard Arrington invited me to write a book about Joseph Smith's early life as the first volume in his projected sixteen-volume history of the Church. That book only took Joseph Smith to the organization of the Church, but I did not think of it as the first stage of a longer biography. After *Joseph Smith and the Beginnings of Mormonism* was completed in 1979 (published in 1984) I immediately went back to work on Massachusetts political culture; *King and People in Provincial Massachusetts* appeared in 1985. In the 1980s I was drawn into studies of material culture through my teaching in the Winterthur Program at the University of Delaware. After completing *The Refinement of America* in the early nineties (I was in my sixties by that time), I briefly considered pursuing my Joseph Smith plan but decided to work on farmers instead. Donna Hill's *Joseph Smith: The First Mormon*, written with the help of her brother Marvin Hill, a Joseph Smith expert, seemed like a biography Mormons could recommend to their friends. What could I add? My wife, Claudia, and I spent our year at the National Humanities Center in North Carolina in 1991-92 working on a farm book we intended to write together. Joseph Smith was turning out to be a youthful dream rather than a life plan.

Not until 1994 when Ronald Esplin, director of the Joseph Fielding Smith Institute for Latter-day Saint History at Brigham Young University, proposed that I write a Joseph Smith biography did I think again. The institute faculty periodically evaluated the state of Mormon studies and had recently concluded that a scholarly biography of the Prophet should be a high priority. Surveying the field again, I realized that none of the biographies portrayed Joseph Smith's religiosity or paid much attention to his thought. The most important part of his life for believing Mormons was left out. After a few months of reflection, I told Ron I would accept. Years later, he backed up his request with a thorough review of every page of the manuscript and a host of useful suggestions. The book would not have been written without his help.

I began working in earnest during a sabbatical at the Huntington Museum and Library in San Marino, California, in 1997. I first thought I would work my way through the materials and write "treatments" of various topics, borrowing a practice of film writers in nearby Hollywood and Burbank. At the end, the treatments would add up to abbreviated pieces of the whole life. I would string them together and write the biography. Claudia was the one to say no to this strategy. I did produce three essays along these lines, but she persuaded me to start writing chapters, beginning where I left off in *Joseph Smith and the Beginnings of Mormonism*.[1] I got started at the Huntington and worked away pretty steadily for seven years.

When I told inquirers in the late nineties that I planned to complete the book in time for Joseph Smith's bicentennial in 2005, they were amused that I was giving myself so much time. They did not understand what it takes to write a history book of any kind, much less a complete biography of a complicated figure like Joseph Smith. Even now I regret that I could not explore his thought more extensively. To do his revelations justice, they should be put in a context of world thought and compared to Augustine, to Milton, to Blake, to Emerson and Bushnell. Not that Joseph Smith was a systematic thinker or originated a new philosophical system, but his insights were original and revolutionary. Many Mormons sense their profundity without knowing how to explain their depth. It will require years of labor by thinkers far more qualified than I to explore their significance.

About halfway through the composition, I began thinking of titles. I wanted something with a little poetic flair, yet descriptive. Fawn Brodie's *No Man Knows My History* had established the possibility of a longish title so I began collecting possible phrases from Joseph's writings. I briefly considered "A Day of Strange Appearances: The Life and Thought of Joseph Smith," taking the first part from a comment of Joseph's in 1832. I weighed more seriously a phrase from Thomas Bullock's notes on the King Follett discourse: "You never knew my heart." But that not only came along in the same paragraph as Brodie's "No Man" but had the same ring. I liked "Rough Stone Rolling" from the start but wondered if people would think of Rolling Stones. In the end, I debated what should come first "Rough Stone Rolling" or "Joseph Smith." In practice the sequence does not seem to matter. People refer to the book as *Rough Stone Rolling*, despite its being second in the title.

The question of the right publisher seemed settled until near the end. I had published *The Refinement of America* with Knopf and Jane Garrett, the editor of their American history books. Knopf is the premier house in the American history field and Jane has a certain genius as an editor. She is light-handed in working with manuscripts, but she ministers to her authors' souls. We had talked for years about the Joseph Smith biography. I told her my book would partially compensate for Knopf's publication of Fawn Brodie's biography in 1945, and she laughingly agreed. (She told me that *No Man Knows My History* still sells a thousand copies a year.) Because I felt so comfortable with Jane and Knopf, I fended off other editors' inquiries—until Bruce Nichols of the Free Press, a subsidiary of Simon and Schuster, approached me. He was more persistent than most, and I finally concluded I might benefit from a reading of a chapter or two by another editor. Nichols did give my pages a good reading, and for a time I thought seriously about switching allegiances. The Free Press even offered an advance that was a third larger than Knopf's. In the end my friendship with Jane and the Knopf name won out, and I returned to my first love.

These negotiations were distractions from finishing the book in time for the 2004 deadline. The manuscript had to be in by the first part of October to be ready for the bicentennial of Joseph Smith's birth in 2005. The book would never have been completed without the assistance of my co-author Jed Woodworth. I hired Jed, then working as an editor at the Joseph Smith Papers at Brigham Young University and soon to begin graduate work at Wisconsin, to source check the book, which entailed looking up every quotation and fact in the original sources to be sure they were accurate, a task it would have taken a year or more to do myself. It turned out that he was an excellent copy editor who improved virtually every paragraph and raised questions about the argument in virtually every chapter. In addition, his knowledge of Mormon historiography far exceeded my own; he was able to direct me to sources I had passed over while writing and to flesh out the notes to cover the most important works. Without his help and Claudia's, my in-house critic, the book would have taken years longer and been a much poorer product.

With all this help, I was still hard pressed to finish by the deadline. Near the end, I was working night and day. I would go to bed with lists of tasks in my mind and wake four hours later to begin again. When I tired, I would nap for an hour and get back to work. The manuscript missed the deadline by a weekend but was delivered to Emily Molanphy, Jane's assistant at Knopf, within a few days of the date in the contract. Claudia and I hand-carried two fat boxes of hard-copy (about 900 pages in all plus illustrations) to Random House headquarters on 56th and Broadway, an easy cab ride from our apartment on 118th and Riverside Drive. I had envisioned walking into the office, plumping down the boxes on Emily's desk, and uttering some wry, triumphant comment. Instead, the guard would not let us even go up to the office. Emily came down, assured us that she could manage, thanked us with a smile, and left. We walked out into the Broadway sunshine carrying a few less pounds than when we entered and confused about what had transpired. Had we passed a watershed in our lives, or was it just one more day in the life of a writer? We could not figure what to do in celebration, so we went for a late breakfast at the Whole Foods Market in the nearby Time-Warner building on 59th.

For the next six months, I was busy answering questions from Emily, reacting to the copy editor's comments, correcting proofs, and compiling the index. The bound galleys, which came along in the spring, achieved an amazing circulation. They went out to scholarly readers for comments for the dust jacket, to review journals, and to an undetermined number of others for purposes I never understood. Collectors asked for copies, and an old friend from Ithaca called to say how much she enjoyed the book—all this more than four months before the publication date.

As my part of the production wound down in the summer of 2005, Glen Nelson, a friend in New York who is impresario for a wide variety of Mormon-related cultural projects, suggested that I keep a running commentary on my experiences as *Joseph Smith: Rough Stone Rolling* came off the press later in the fall.   Glen publishes art in many forms through Mormon Artists Group—exhibits, performances, and books—and he thought the story of an author and a book might interest readers. I took Glen to mean I should record my reaction to the reviews, books signings, and talks that would inevitably follow in the months after publication on September 27. A book I had labored on for seven years was going public; how did I feel about it? Since I have worked all my life with other people's records, it seemed fitting to make a record of my own to deposit in the great trough where the raw materials of the world's history are kept. In July 2005, I began making diary entries about the flow of events.

I begin the story as I sent off the last proofs to the printer and almost simultaneously as the first review of the bound galleys came in. Fortunately, the first review (by Jeffrey Needle) was positive, giving me hope that my work was not in vain. But it was only the beginning. Reviews of all kind, both public and private, kept arriving through the fall, and on top of these I got scores of email messages, letters, and personal comments from people at book signings and talks. Since the comments that came to me were almost all favorable, I was heavy on the positive and light on the negative. That helped balance my reaction when Larry McMurtry wrote a disparaging review for the *New York Review of Books*. McMurtry did not pan the book so much as deride Joseph Smith, eliciting a storm of protest from my scholarly friends which daunted him not a bit. Meanwhile, I went from one Church group to another speaking about the Prophet, occasionally appearing at university seminars and historical societies along the way. All of that is jumbled together in the diary entries.

So far I have not sorted out the experience of writing about Joseph Smith or suddenly being thrust into the limelight during the bicentennial celebration. As the months went by, I tried to put everything into perspective, but it is still a confusing whirl. I have encountered too many reactions, received too much praise, heard too many criticisms, thought too many thoughts to make sense of it all now. The diary is raw material for someone else to comprehend. I feel like a player in the Mormon cultural scene who only vaguely knows his part.

Richard Bushman
New York City
August 2006

Notes

[1] The three later appeared as *Making Space for the Mormons* (Logan: Special Collections and Archives, Merrill-Cazier Library, Utah State University, 1997); "The Visionary World of Joseph Smith," *BYU Studies* 31, no. 1 (1997–98): 183–204; and "Joseph Smith as Translator," in *The Prophet Puzzle: Interpretive Essays on Joseph Smith*, edited by Bryan Waterman (Salt Lake City: Signature Books, 1999): 69–86.

The Diaries

Preparations: July–August 2005

July 12, 2005

The third-pass galleys left for New York last Thursday. I turned them around in less than twenty-four hours, keeping up my record for punctuality. Usually authors do not see the third pass at all, save for the index which was constructed from the pagination in the second pass (following the corrections made in the first pass). But a few questions had arisen in the body of the work requiring one more look. I was under strict instructions from my Knopf editor Jane Garrett: "no rewriting!!!!!!!!" Of course, I could not resist a few stylistic alterations. I remembered Jane's genial observation that Laurel Ulrich kept making changes in *A Midwife's Tale* right down to the end. That licensed me to tinker. Fortunately, the prose sounded all right this time. Sometimes my writing, even after much revision, sounds gummy. But I let the text leave my hands for the last time with few regrets. Those doubtless will come later when critics speak.

The book is now in the hands of fate. I am told that my daughter-in-law Harriet Bushman, who hears a few pages each night as my son Brick reads to her, refers to the book as "RSR." Not bad. From her British lips it sounds a little like HRH. I would not mind if it came to be known as "Rough Stone Rolling." I debated to the end whether to put "Joseph Smith" first or second in the title. My friendly adviser, Jim Lucas, was all for putting "Rough Stone Rolling" first, as was I slightly. But other consultants recommended the reverse, and the editors did not weigh in with an opinion. If people pick up the second title as the working description, I will be happy.

I have no idea what to expect from here on. Elizabeth Cochrane, the publicist at Knopf, tells me that Deseret Book has ordered 10,000 copies, which she says is huge. Deseret Book wants to sponsor a reception in the Joseph Smith Memorial Building at the end of October. My first reaction when I hear a number like that is to calculate how many books Knopf must sell to recover the advance. I don't want to fall short. Of course, I start making money at that point too, but strangely I am more worried about getting to the break-even point than going ahead. I estimate they must sell a minimum of 15,000 copies and probably more like 20,000. I am not quite interested enough to make an exact calculation based on my royalties, but the thought does come to mind.

How the book will be received remains up in the air. I know a lot of Mormons are interested, but will they be surprised or put off? I have given talks about some of the more or less controversial portions of the book to a variety of audiences— the Sons of the Utah Pioneers national encampment in Philadelphia last Saturday—and it seemed to work. Elder Oaks liked my talk "Joseph Smith's Many Histories" at the Library of Congress symposium last May, and Elder Marlin Jensen raised no objections to my paper "The Inner Joseph Smith" given at the Mormon History Association in Killington, Vermont.[1] As for non-Mormons and especially the scholarly critics, I am ready for a mixed response. George Marsden, the Notre Dame evangelical scholar who was asked to write a blurb for the dust jacket, replied that I had written the definitive biography for Mormons and a defense of the revelations, but not a book for others. That stung me. I had hoped a book suitable for Mormons could be enlightening for others. Apparently not. I am sure I will get stuck with the tag "apologist." The word makes it sound as if I will bend the evidence to protect Joseph Smith no matter what. My reply is that the equivalent term for other kinds of biographers should then be "cynic," those who will resort to any tactics to discredit Joseph Smith. Neither term is fair to the motives or the result. I have told the story as I see it. I haven't bent the evidence. I have tried to see the world as Joseph Smith saw it. Is that apologetic? I would do the same for Mohammad or Charles Finney.

July 15, 2005

Jed Woodworth sent me the first formal review of *RSR*. Jeffrey Needle, a person I know only vaguely, reviewed it for the Association for Mormon Letters. It was definitely friendly, laudatory in almost all respects. Needle said if the writings on Joseph Smith are likened to a football field, I am squarely on the fifty-yard line. I discounted the praise because the AML is basically a faithful—though candid—group. Needle did not object to my in-favor bias. From more critical people, like the evangelicals, I can expect much worse. The strange thing is I did not want to read the review, even after the laudatory opening paragraph. I feel uncomfortable being examined in public, for good or ill. I can see I have to become hardened. We all know that reviews say as much about the reviewer as the book. Needle probably wanted a positive biography of Joseph and gave me credit for providing one. Those who want Joseph hanged will object to my gentle treatment.

Here are a few excerpts:

> Bushman, author of a previous, and well-received, biography of the Prophet, devoted years to expanding and updating that book (*Joseph Smith and the Beginnings of Mormonism*). He and his wife, Claudia, are well-known in the Mormon community for both their writing and their public speaking.

> The challenge he faces has more to do with his heart than with his head. As a self-professed "believing Mormon," he runs the risk of favoring faithful history over the evidential

testimony. Often this is a matter of sifting through the available evidence, deciding some points are more relevant than others, and constructing an apologetic that does not reflect the larger picture. On the other hand, enemies of the church can likewise sift and sort, producing a very different picture of the Mormon institution and its leadership.

Bushman takes a modified middle road—that is, he makes an effort to acknowledge the controversial aspects of the life of this very controversial figure, and places them alongside the more positive aspects, nearly always coming down on the side of the faithfully supportive.

This, of course, is to be expected—this is what faithful writers do. But I give him great credit in that he presents the story in all its richness—warts and all—rather than pretend that the warts aren't there. By doing so, he adds the veneer of credibility to his writing.

July 16, 2005

Jed Woodworth, my co-author who sent me the review, was struck by Needle's delight that Mormons are finally being told the truth and wondered "how many Mormons feel as though the church has been deceiving them." Jed reported that a friend in the Mormon publishing business "proclaimed that he was going to buy 10 copies and pass them out to conservative Mormon relatives." That idea worried me a little. Are all the liberals going to wave the book under the noses of their conservative fellow members and say "I told you so"?

August 9, 2005

[Quincy Newell, a teacher of religion at the University of Wyoming, raised some questions about faith and history in an email exchange just before the book appeared. Quincy attended the summer seminar on Joseph Smith run by Grant Underwood and me for the National Endowment for the Humanities at Brigham Young University in 2005. A Presbyterian and recent graduate from the Religion Department at University of North Carolina, she was personally concerned about how to integrate her own Christian faith with her scholarship. She was intrigued that I was so blatant in *Believing History*, a collection of my Mormon essays that she was reviewing. An excerpt from her letter and my reply went into the diary because the questions she raises about *Believing History* apply to *Joseph Smith: Rough Stone Rolling*.]

Dear Richard,

I've been thinking about *Believing History* a lot lately, because I've been reviewing it (along with two other books) for *Church History*. I sent the review off today (I'll be happy to send you a copy, if you like), but the book raised some questions for me that I've not yet resolved, so I thought I would email you about them. (In other words, I'm going to make them your problem too . . .)

The second section of the book ("The Book of Mormon and History") was where I ran into difficulties. I found myself surprised to see you taking the Book of Mormon as what it claims to be (that is, as an ancient record of the inhabitants of the Americas)—and then I was surprised at my surprise, because it stands to reason that a believing Mormon would believe the book's claims to historicity. Once I'd gotten over all this surprise, I was left with the dilemma of what to do with these essays, proceeding as they do from a premise to which I do not subscribe. As a religious studies scholar, and as a believing historian myself, I want to affirm that one's religious convictions have a place in one's scholarship. But the (secular) historian in me insists that the same standards of verifiability ought to apply to sacred texts, when they are used for historical purposes, as apply to other texts. I'm not up on all the scholarship, but my understanding is that there is little or no corroborative evidence for the narrative in the Book of Mormon.

For the purposes of my review, I simply said that the essays in that section would have limited appeal to scholars who don't buy the historicity of the Book of Mormon but pointed out that even those scholars may glean interesting insights into the book from the essays in that section. But I would be interested in your views on this topic—because what I seem to be saying is that, in the end, maybe my faith doesn't have a place in the academy, or that my faith is okay as long as I don't work on topics like the life of Jesus. And that doesn't satisfy me.

I should tell you that apart from this dilemma, I really liked the book. I found the first section interesting and thought-provoking (and even faith promoting), and the last section was, I thought, full of brilliant insights. I particularly liked "Making Space for the Mormons" and the essay on the rhetoric of revelation. The latter, I thought, never fully answered the questions it raised, but I find the questions interesting enough that I'm satisfied to not have complete answers.

I would be interested in your (further) thoughts on faith and scholarship or in knowing what you thought about as you put that middle section of *Believing History* together. And if you would like a copy of my review, let me know— I'll send it to you.

I hope all's well—

Quincy

Dear Quincy:

Your question is not out of line with the review of *Believing History* in *Books and Culture.* You are asking, as the earlier reviewer did, how can a reasonable historian even pretend the events of the Book of Mormon were true? That is a fact of life for all Mormons all the time. They live with the realization that much of the world they believe to exist is nonsense for everyone else. It is disorienting for Mormons to live that way, and now I am discovering it is disorienting for non-Mormons who think they understand their Mormon friends but then realize they don't. There is some perplexing disjuncture in Mormon brains. As you say it is potentially a problem for any believing Christian, but is more sharply enunciated for Mormons. You must remember that within the walls of Mormonism all sorts of reasonable, functioning, educated people believe the Book of Mormon. That of course helps a Mormon to remain sane. It is also why many Mormons like myself have a post-modern turn to their minds. We, more than most others, recognize how socially constructed truth is. It really is what people agree to believe—or what methods of ascertaining truth they concur in. If you go inside the Mormon community, you find all sort of reasons for accepting the historical authenticity of the Book of Mormon. It is not at all a one-sided case. One quite well-respected Mormon archeologist is now claiming there is actually more archeological evidence for the Book of Mormon than for the Old and New Testaments. That is a contested conclusion, of course, but it is not an empty claim.

So you see the fact is that Mormon intellectuals live in two worlds that touch and overlap and can converse but which are structured in quite different ways. I actually have rather complicated ways of thinking about the Book of Mormon, but they do come down to the belief that it is true. Personally I think that it is possible that Joseph's inspiration led him to interpret the ancient text for a modern audience, for that is what all prophets do. They explain old texts for new circumstances.

One reason *Believing History* is disorienting is that you and other non-Mormon readers were not the intended audience for the original essays. Virtually everything in the collection was written for Mormons. Some of the essays have pious endings. They were not meant to persuade non-believers to accept Mormon premises. They start with the premises Mormons accept and work on the implications. The book is not apologetics but explorations. My ideal reader would look on as an observer of the species Mormona. What are the folkways of their intellectuals? What concerns them? How do they deal with intellectual issues? The correct response is not acceptance or rejection but reflections on the peculiarities of Mormon thought.

I wish I could strike a responsive chord in Christians like you. Mormons wonder why all Christians don't understand that we believe in the Book of Mormon on the basis of a spiritual witness. It is very hard for a Mormon to believe that Christians accept the Bible because of the scholarly evidence confirming the historical accuracy of the work. Surely there are uneducated believers whose convictions are not rooted in academic knowledge. Isn't there some kind of human, existential truth that resonates with one's desires for goodness and divinity? And isn't that ultimately why we read the Bible as a devotional work? We don't have to read the latest issues of the journals to find out if the book is still true. We stick with it because we find God in its pages—or inspiration, or comfort, or scope. That is what religion is about in my opinion, and it is why I believe the Book of Mormon. I can't really evaluate all the scholarship all the time; while I am waiting for it to settle out, I have to go on living. I need some good to hold on to and to lift me up day by day. The Book of Mormon inspires me, and so I hold on.

Reason is too frail to base a life on. You can be whipped about by all the authorities with no genuine basis for deciding for yourself. I think it is far better to go where goodness lies.

I keep thinking other Christians are in a similar position, but they don't agree. They keep insisting their beliefs are based on reason and evidence. I can't buy that—the resurrection as rational fact? And so I am frankly as perplexed about Christian belief as you are about Mormons. Educated Christians claim to base their belief on reason when I thought faith was the teaching of the scriptures. You hear the Good Shepherd's voice, and you follow it.

I guess we could go on and on. I hope I am telling you the truth about myself. The fact is I am a believer and I can't help myself. I couldn't possibly give it up; it is too delicious.

Richard

August 17, 2005

Yesterday we attended the wedding of Jansen Gates and Bart Bradshaw in the Salt Lake Temple followed by an elaborate wedding lunch in the Empire Room of the Joseph Smith Memorial Building and later a reception at the house of Bart's mother's father. At the reception, the bride's father, my brother-in-law Crawford Gates, asked about the book as everyone does. He wanted to know the print run, a figure I have not been given. He spoke of high anticipation, which is indeed a fact. Everyone seems to know about the biography and promises to purchase it. My first reaction is doubt about meeting the expectations, and uncertainty about how high the sales will be. What kind of reaction do you expect, Crawford wanted to know. Mixed, I replied honestly. There are people who don't like Mormonism and don't like religion who will slam the book as a whitewash. Others will find it illuminating. Judging from the Jeffrey Needle review, some potential critics will be disarmed by my candor—the "veneer of credibility," Needle called it. They will be surprised that a believer deals with as many problems as I do. But others will find damning facts I pass over or fail to give due weight. The *Library Journal* review was basically positive though it only "recommended" the book, not grading it "highly recommended." The good thing: it was recommended for academic and public libraries.

August 24, 2005

Last week a few facts about the book came in the email. Jane Garrett forwarded some Knopf internal exchanges on the print run. Costco had upped its order from 3,000 to 6,000 books for sale in its Utah and Mormon stores. Costco! Reminded me of seeing the latest Harry Potter book in Smith's supermarket. So I am to become a bargain basement author. I am complimented and amused. In Mormondom, of course, they may sell a few copies. The email said the Knopf people increased order for books just as the Costco request came in going from 35,000 to 40,000 books. That struck me as a high number.

I read the *Library Journal* review again—only twenty or thirty lines. The chief complaint was that the book is not critical enough. I am sure that will come up over and over. People are accustomed to Joseph Smith the scalawag. A true account, some think, will show him to be sly and brash. I remain too consistently sympathetic for readers who want their authors to take a dig or two at this pious fraud. On the other hand, Mormons will be upset in places about my candor. I suppose that is exactly where I want to be, though I am disappointed at the cynicism of so many readers. They must have a Joseph who is at least part scoundrel.

August 24, 2005

[A *Los Angeles Times* religion reporter named William Lobdell asked me to answer a few questions about Joseph Smith for an article on "the drumroll leading up to the 200th anniversary of Joseph Smith's birth." About this time I began to realize the need for brief answers to difficult questions, a kind of extended sound bite.]

Dear Mr. Lobdell:

Here are a few words in answer to your questions.

1. *How is Joseph Smith seen by Mormons?*

Mormons take the Bible literally. They believe that God spoke to the prophets when the book was first written and that he speaks to them now. In Mormon eyes, when Joseph Smith began receiving revelations, he reenacted the writing of the Bible. He stood in the great tradition of biblical prophecy going back to Adam and the Patriarchs, down through Moses and Isaiah, to Christ's apostles. That conviction anchors Mormon faith. Mormons have been less affected by skepticism because their modern prophet has revitalized their belief.

2. *What does the bicentennial celebration mean to Mormons?*

The bicentennial of Joseph Smith's birth has been a time for Mormons to take stock. They want to take the measure of the man themselves, but they are also interested in how he is regarded by the world at large. Is he finally winning respect, or is he still considered to be no more than an imaginative fraud? It is hard for Mormons to understand why teachings that inspire them are so easily dismissed by non-Mormons. Shouldn't Joseph Smith at least be given the respect afforded to other religious leaders and Christian visionaries?

3. *Why was Joseph Smith polarizing?*

The reaction to Joseph Smith is not that much different from the response to prophetic figures throughout history. Prophets demand too much of people. They require them to believe in the miraculous and, if they believe, to change their lives. Moreover, prophets threaten social equanimity. They seem dangerous, verging too close to the fanatic for comfort. Fearing that fanatics will break down conventional morality, citizens often resort to violence to halt the fanatics' course. Mormons suffered from persecution wherever they settled, largely because people worried about them taking over society and forcing their beliefs on everyone else. Every effort of Joseph Smith to prove his toleration of all religions was in vain. People still felt they had to drive the Mormons out.

I hope you find something you can use.

Richard Bushman

August 27, 2005

Martha Cox Ballantyne called last night from Ithaca. I knew Martha when she was a teenager in Belmont and I was a student at Harvard. Her husband, an MIT student when he met her, took her to Cornell where he had a distinguished career as a scientist and vice-president of research. I think she called just to tell me she liked the biography. She somehow had wangled a copy of the bound galleys by invoking her husband's position. This year she is teaching an LDS Institute class at Cornell and plans to use the biography. She is an enthusiast by nature but was certainly happy with the book. I told her I was pleased with her reaction because she is the ideal Mormon reader—believing, informed, independent. If she liked the book, so will many other Mormons. I have worried that it would disappoint some Mormon readers because it presents a Joseph with flaws and struggles. That may be just the kind of Joseph educated Mormons want to know.

Notes

1 Both talks were later published. "Joseph Smith's Many Histories," *BYU Studies* 44, no. 4 (2005): 3–20; and "The Inner Joseph Smith," *Journal of Mormon History* 32, no. 1 (Spring 2006): 65–81.

On Tour: September–December 2005

September 2, 2005

Emily Molanphy called from Knopf yesterday to ask if I would be home to receive copies of my book. About 5:15 that afternoon the messenger arrived with a big envelope containing four copies. Sitting on the bed, I cut open the package, and there they were. I felt numb. Neither rejoicing nor regrets. Claudia and I sat and read parts here and there. I read the jacket copy which Jed and I had labored over for days. It was okay. The same with the concluding pages. Nothing to make me cringe. The book will do. The only error I found was the citation to Jonathan Edwards's *History of the Work of Redemption*. The bibliography cites the old 1805 edition rather than the modern 1989 edition. I had run on to this problem earlier in the day while writing an essay for the Charles Warren Center. It is not a big deal. Now the four books are standing like sentinels on the front bureau. One goes off to Jed today. Another to Jim Lucas who read many chapters for me. Emily said I will get twenty copies eventually.

What do I have to say about this milestone? Nothing. The book will have to fend for itself. I expect to be criticized in the *New York Times* and scores of other public places for being too orthodox, too partial, too celebratory. Mormons may be more accepting than I had thought. The favorable reception of Greg Prince's biography of David O. McKay makes me think there is an audience of educated Mormons waiting for a sensible rendition of Church history. They will like my kind of balance. Laurel Ulrich wrote yesterday asking me to write an essay for the online historical journal

Common-Place. She wanted to know what question I would address; I said, What does it mean to write a balanced book? By the time the essay is due next June, I should have plenty to say on the subject.

Claudia's first response was to ask how we can celebrate. "I will buy you an ice cream cone," she suggested. We went to an overly long production of Bertold Brecht's Mother Courage at the Bowerie Theater on Play by Play tickets that cost about $3 each. That was a mild celebration. Today she is going to order a big supply of groceries. That's good, too. Actually I can't think of a way to celebrate except to keep on plugging. I got an email from an editor at the French journal *Annales: Economies, Sociétés, Civilisations* about an essay on agriculture. I had forgotten that I had agreed to write something on the North and South in the eighteenth century for a special issue. That will give me something to work on next winter and return my attention to farming.

September 4, 2005

Glen Nelson wrote a paragraph in an email this morning that brought me peculiar pleasure: "I went to Knopf's website to see when the book is due, and I came across the press release. Now that's a beautifully written document! And those early reviews are just wonderful." I find myself responding most to compliments about the writing. Jed and I labored over the press release which is actually just the jacket copy. That Glen, a writer, likes it made me happy. I went to the Knopf website to follow up and found another review, this one for *Publisher's Weekly*, which was written, if my information is correct, by Jana Riess, an old friend. The reviewer, whoever it was, spoke well of the writing in the book. Again another little buzz of pleasure. I lugged a copy of the book to church this morning in a plain brown wrapper to give to Jim Lucas. He was happy to have it. On the inscription I wrote how much I appreciated his acute suggestions. He did help out. In priesthood meeting, I met a visitor named Ralph Tate from Holladay, Utah. When I gave him my name, he said something about my being famous. That surprises me. Where did my notoriety come from? Four or five years ago, my name was not particularly well known. My appearance on Lee Groberg's *American Prophet* video may have reached a wide audience of Mormons. They apparently play the video over and over on BYU-TV. I make four or five brief appearances along with a half dozen or so other talking heads.

Going back to the Knopf website, I linked from their home page to various online booksellers. I discovered that Barnes and Noble sells the book for $28, seven dollars below Knopf's price, Amazon for $23 something, and Wal-Mart, that old devil, for $21, advertised as a 39 percent discount. You can see why all the retailers resent that behemoth; they undersell everyone. Did they squeeze Knopf to get the price down that far, or do they work on very low margins?

While waiting for patriarchal blessings this afternoon, I sat in the church lobby outlining my talk for the Massachusetts Historical Society next month, the same address I will give at the Princeton-Columbia club a week later. My talk to the Columbia University senior faculty (retired) a few years back persuaded me I can say something to interest educated outsiders. We will see how these talks go. My rules are: (1) make a few clear, numbered points, so the audience knows what I am doing; (2) scatter arresting facts and insights through the piece.

September 8, 2005

Little scraps of feedback keep fluttering my way. Dennis Lythgoe of the *Deseret News* interviewed me over the phone for about an hour yesterday. An old friend from Boston days, he earlier wrote a big spread on Claudia and me. This time he will do the same on me for the Arts Section front page with a book review on the second. All this happens on September 18, a week before the book is due in the stores. What could make Knopf happier? Dennis was very complimentary as was Jim Lucas to whom I gave a copy on Sunday as thanks for reading chapters. I am getting enough feedback to be convinced many Mormons will be happy with the book. Dennis wanted to know if I expected criticism from the General Authorities. I have no idea.

I also heard from a person planning a meeting for LDS chaplains that I had been invited to address. He reported that his advisers had turned down his nomination of me as a speaker. Was that a sign of something? I can see resistance on the grounds of my becoming too much of an authority on the Prophet. Whether or not they agree with the book, the General Authorities don't like someone like me taking control of interpretation. They objected to FARMS on those grounds after they seemed to be monopolizing Book of Mormon interpretation. The Brethren become uneasy when someone gets too many readers. I can envision a cancellation of the big party Deseret Book is planning for October 27 in the Joseph Smith Memorial Building. That comes too close to an endorsement.

I put a copy of the book in the mail to Elder Holland a few days ago. He can give the Authorities his reaction. Many of these brethren will not be thrilled with what I write, but I do have a history of winning people over because of my kindly spirit. I know I will have supporters among a few General Authorities, but they may not be in a position to speak up if the book comes under attack.

September 13, 2005

Little bits of acclaim come in from time to time. Yesterday Jane Garrett sent me a copy of the Knopf publicity release, basically a page of quotations from favorable reviews and the blurbs sent in by scholars like the ones on the back of the dust jacket. I can picture the book getting a fair amount of praise, especially from Latter-day Saints. But each of these little bits of praise reminds me that I will be subject to public humiliation too. I keep thinking of the *New York Times* review when it comes. More likely than not, it will go to someone who thinks Joseph Smith was a scoundrel and the Mormons fanatics. There are lots of people like that in the world, and lots of them have opined on Mormonism. They will think my book is a celebration and anything but a balanced history. My works and I will be demeaned in the public prints. It could have happened when *Joseph Smith and the Beginnings of Mormonism* was published but didn't, mainly because the book was small potatoes. This full-length biography, published by Knopf and persuasive in its way, will be more of a threat. Reviewers will have to knock it down because it stands up to their point of view. The Harvard religious historian Robert Orsi, who also writes empathetically, has observed that his critics object to his sympathetic portrayals of people's religious faith and practices. The fact that he is a substantial scholar with standing in the profession makes him all the more dangerous and annoying to the skeptics.

Why do I care about this? I worry that my friends in the Church will see their friend and champion struck down and bleeding. They may be crushed when they see that I cannot vanquish the disbelievers. They will lament the foul treatment and sympathize, but they will be less courageous as a result. They may worry that they may be hurt, too. If they cannot be protected in their faith, are they safe? This will be a minuscule event in their faith history, but it troubles me nonetheless. I will have fallen short. I have always feared that I will disappoint people.

Emily Molanphy in response to my question said that Knopf will send out copies of the books to scholars. That relieves me of the cost and trouble of mailing the book to all those who read chapters or helped in other ways. I still have debts to pay with the twenty copies I am to get, but I am happy to give out copies to people who lent me a hand.

Today I hope to finish up my paper for the Claremont Graduate University conference "Joseph Smith and the Prophetic Tradition" next month. Finish the draft, that is. The revisions will go on for a while. I am supposed to lay down the basis for the next day's discussion in my keynote address "Joseph Smith and the Creation of the Sacred." The following morning, two other scholars will discuss Mohammad and Ellen G. White in comparison to Joseph Smith. My thesis is that Joseph Smith's influence arose from his capacity for putting people in touch with the sacred, a gift that he must have shared with other prophets.

I am coming to take hope from the revising process. I am writing in a rush these days, starting out with a bare outline and scarcely consulting it as I go. I write what seems to flow naturally from the previous work. At the end I have a rough-hewn draft that may not make its points clearly. The argument emerges only as I revise. I had this experience with the Library of Congress paper last spring.[1] I kept asking myself, What is the interesting point in the paper? Gradually it became clear; and by tweaking and tinkering, I brought it out. Strangely the paper has gotten good reviews. Not just people at the conference but viewers of the rebroadcast comment on its interest, when I thought it was a little abstruse and complicated. I hope to get the same results with the other talks I am giving. I am getting them written out but certainly not finished. I sense they are lumbering and bulgy but I will keep asking myself, "What is interesting here?" In a way I am outlining after writing rather than before. I write down the key points and then go back to the prose to make it say what I want it to say. For some reason, my mind goes to the idea of a God in time. We often say that about Joseph Smith's God: He is not outside of time, which means I guess that he accomplishes his works in sequence, one step at a time. That is the message of the creation stories. It takes time to make the earth. We should, I assume, think about our lives the same way. We are not perfect in a day. We don't get everything right at the beginning. We have to plug along, growing from grace to grace. Perhaps in philosophical terms this means essences don't matter. It is not what we are but what we are becoming that counts. We have to keep making ourselves, or ask God to make us, like carpenters building houses, joining one stick to another.

September 14, 2005

Spent the day on the Princeton Club talk on Joseph Smith, also scheduled for early next month in the peak season for public appearances. My announced topic is "The Many Lives of Joseph Smith." I have asked Kim Smith, Area General Authority, Olene and Myron Walker, New York public affairs missionaries, along with two friends, Mark Holden and Jim Lucas, to the dinner beforehand. I am having trouble putting the talk together. I had thought the Massachusetts Historical Society talk would overlap this one, but that paper has taken a decidedly New England bent. I am not sure it will work at Princeton. While writing I try to follow my inspiration, which means listening to signals that I am heading off on the wrong track. The signals kept coming today. I stopped and started a half dozen times and began to feel desperate. Then at lunch I started to sense where to go. I jotted down the outline and it flowed freely, though I still am not absolutely certain I am striking the right note. I have a tendency to be too diffident and overly modest. Claudia hates that. I intend to confront the gold plates problem head on, the foundation for thinking of Joseph Smith as a fraud.

September 15, 2005

Woke up this morning filled with anxiety. Can I write that Princeton talk? I came in about 5:30 and roughed in an outline on two pages of blank paper. Reassured myself. There is something there to say. Lacks a slam bang ending—always the hard part—but makes sense. A little concerned the outline will fall apart on me like all the previous ones. But it is getting better. As I said before, I have to work in time, letting the pieces fall in place one by one. A few improved touches on this version. That is all I can hope for—a touch here and there. Pretty soon it will be okay. Today we work at the temple. Maybe that will clear my mind.

September 19, 2005

Jim Lucas suggested to the New York Stake History Committee meeting at our apartment last night that there be a big book signing for *RSR*. I drag my feet and hold back. He loves the book—a page-turner he says. I know it is going to be given only grudging respect in many of the reviews. There will not be the excitement and enthusiasm Jim and others expect. When I think about the prospects, I feel sober not exultant. I haven't quite kept the non-Mormon audience with me. This leads me to read trouble into nothing. I imagine that Knopf is pulling back a tad. They are not promoting the book as hard as they promised to do at first. No book signings in New York other than the Princeton Club which I arranged on my own. In fact they have not arranged for any signings except at Deseret Book. They can already smell the blood in the water. It will not be enthusiastically received followed by big sales, so cut the losses. I haven't heard from the publicist for weeks. I am left dangling on my own. Could I have written a book the critics would have liked better? Possibly. Terryl Givens might have been able to do it. He has a knack for hiding his preferences and sounding more balanced. My enthusiasms show through. I might have voiced the criticism more thoroughly the way he does. I feel myself hunkering down, waiting for the blows to fall. The friends of Joseph Smith will like the book; the critics will be critical. I am afraid the biography will be for the Latter-day Saints and no one else.

Mark Holden, a banker and member of the stake history committee, has suggested I could possibly get a tax break for my papers. He thinks they are worth something. The early versions of the manuscript along with Jed's corrections are sitting in three boxes on the dining room floor. He thinks in time they would be worth $25,000 on the collectors' market—more after the book has been out for a while and established itself. He advised holding the boxes for a few years and then giving them to BYU. I nodded my head as my eyes glazed over. I am sure there is some truth to this. I will write Roy Ritchie at the Huntington and see what kind of a figure he would assign. Mark thinks Curt Bench would have an idea of their worth. All of this rings hollow as I question whether the book will make its way in the world at all.

September 22, 2005

Elizabeth Cochrane, the book's publicist at Knopf, called to ask if I had given any interviews lately. I could only remember Dennis Lythgoe's call and the prospect of a *Deseret News* article next Sunday. Next week I am to talk to the Associated Press reporter in Salt Lake. That was all. She said they were puzzled to see that Amazon orders had increased. You mean by twenty or thirty? I asked, thinking of Grant Underwood's plan to order copies for last summer's NEH seminar participants. No, many more, she says. Amazon ranks its books by the number of orders received. I had been up in the thousands somewhere. Suddenly I rose to 190th. How to explain it, I cannot say. It could only be some kind of fluke. I went online to see the number for myself but couldn't find it. She also said the Church Public Affairs office had been talking to her about the book. That surprised me. What can they do? I hope that Elder Holland has looked at the volume I sent him. Otherwise they are promoting a pig in a poke. My reactions have brought out the peculiarities of my character. When I talk to Claudia about my fears and reservations, she says how much better off I am with this book than most Church authors. She wants to assure me that I am ranked high. My great fear is disappointment. I am supposed to deliver and don't. That is the explanation for the false modesty that covers my vanity. I don't want to appear bigger than I am for fear of disappointing.

I finally did find the ranking number at Amazon. It was #761 today and #675 yesterday. So it's a highly variable number. A surge of orders comes in and the ranking rises. That's not a bad number anyway for a book not published and reviewed.

September 23, 2005

[I had written Jed Woodworth that "I know I will get lambasted in very public places. But JS did too, so why not me?" Jed wrote his view of the risks.]

Hey, that's the right attitude. The marvelous thing is you have a second chance—the 2d ed—to answer the lambast if you so choose. I am a little uneasy myself. The fact checker is never recognized for what he does right, only for what he does wrong. If I goofed someone will point it out (and, to be sure, I have already started my own short list). Then there is the question of my public stance. Times and Seasons [an internet blog] had wanted me to comment on the book but then backed away when they realized I was "too partial," as they said, neither author nor a critic. Fine by me. They could see I was in a kind of no-man's-land and I was happy to get out of the request. Still, they want me to comment when the reviews go up. What do I say about interpretations that aren't mine? How much do I say about the evolution of this sentence or that? Do you have any advice—I want to be loyal in all instances.

jw

[My reply:]

Okay, we both have cases of pre-review jitters. They will come and go, wash over us, and then be gone. The book will take on its own life no matter what we or anyone else does. You are in a delicate situation: not the author yet complicit. The words that come into my mind for your response to critics are: "This is what I think the book tries to do." Not you or me, but the book. I think we can talk candidly about where it falls short too. Heavens knows we thought it was a rushed operation when we were writing it. It could have been better with five years more work. On the other hand, we want to include ourselves among those who can pull the trigger, as John Kaminski puts it.

Richard

September 24, 2005

Elizabeth Cochrane has an explanation for the spike in Amazon sales the other day. As a book's publication date draws near, Amazon sends a message to people who have bought books on Mormonism to tell them a new book is ready. It is a clever idea, the bookstore equivalent of browsing; while looking for one book, you pick up another. Knopf mailed me a short review from Booklist. Basically favorable. I realize I don't like to read any kind of review, even the favorable ones. I am annoyed by what the reviewers choose to

emphasize in Joseph's life. Most of them pick up a few frag-
ments and present them as if they were the key elements.
There is something so cavalier about the implicit assertion that
they have delivered the essence of the man.

September 26, 2005

I got mixed up about fast meeting yesterday and mistakenly
fasted. It turns out fast day is the Sunday after general conference rather than the Sunday before. As I awoke in the morning, it struck me that I should bear testimony to thank God for
help with the book. I sought a blessing from Elder Packer
before getting started; and insofar as I was worthy, I think the
blessing was fulfilled. Midway in the writing I began to wonder where my ideas came from. After I had absorbed all the
basic sources for a chapter, the themes and organization would
just come to me. I got the facts through my eyes by reading,
but where did the ideas come from? I felt like a person sitting
by a fire in the woods in the dark night. Out of the dark for-
est, figures emerged into the light. Where they came from, I
could not say. Ideas come to everyone in the same way, I think,
but the process was more evident to me because it was happening day after day. I hope that inspiration played a part in
forming the figures who appeared. In my unborne testimony,
I wanted to express appreciation and to say I believe the Holy
Spirit can help all of us to get the right ideas.

I am beginning to panic about all these talks I am giving. The
ones I read should not be difficult, but for others I am just talking and still not completely confident about the structure.
With three more days before the onslaught begins, I awoke
this morning with my stomach in a knot. These talks will test
my theories about acting in time. The idea is if you keep working at something, it improves incrementally. As you apply your
mind, one thought after another comes along to strengthen the
organization and the argument. I will have time on the air-

planes to go over the outlines, tightening them up, as my old teacher Bernard Bailyn used to say, to emphasize the critical points and clarify the murky. Still and all, I feel I am exercising pure faith. I must have inspiration or I will not survive. The big exposure points: Massachusetts Historical Society, Harvard's Charles Warren Center seminar, and the Princeton Club, all within a few days of one another in early October.

September 28, 2005

Yesterday the book was formally published. Reid Neilson called with congratulations and said there must have been 400 copies stacked in the BYU Bookstore. Jed Woodworth wrote asking what Claudia and I were doing to celebrate. I said, Go to the opera. We actually hadn't thought about it. When we did, we decided we would go to dinner beforehand. Claudia's sister Georgia Gates had given us gift certificates to a little restaurant across the street from Lincoln Center. I had a curried chicken sandwich and Claudia a specialty plate with ricotta cheese and pesto sauce which we wolfed down because were a little late for a 7:30 performance of *Patience* at City Opera. I walked out with a piece of French bread slathered with ricotta and finished the last bite just as we reached the front doors of the New York State Theater. When *From Puritan to Yankee* was published in 1967, Harvard University Press sent Claudia a dozen roses. The old days. Not a peep from Knopf yesterday. They are not into celebrations any more than we are. I called Elder Packer's office about how to deliver a copy to him when I am in Salt Lake next week. When I was getting started, he gave me photocopies of the introduction to a nineteenth-century *Life of Christ* by Frederic Farrar, a believing Christian. He proposed Farrar's attitude as a model for a believing historian. I want to give Elder Packer a signed copy to round out the sequence and express appreciation. He may not feel I have lived up to the Farrar standard.

When I finished making this entry, I opened my email and found a short note from Dean Jessee, general editor of the Joseph Smith Papers, labeled "Dancing in the Streets."

Dear Richard,

A word of gratitude for the book I found when I arrived at my office this morning. It brightened up my whole universe—even without your kind words of dedication. It is an important day for the church to finally have a biography of Joseph Smith we can trust and feel good about recommending.

Your writings have been a great inspiration to me; may the Lord continue to bless you,

Dean

PS—As I passed through Deseret Book this evening on my way to the bus there were stacks of the biography all over the place; it looks like they are planning for a big invasion.

My reaction to this nice little note: Will he feel the same way after he has read it? Will Deseret Book be stuck with a pile of books they cannot sell? The old fear of disappointing.

September 29, 2005

St. Louis, Day's Inn, 11:00 p.m., New York time. The flight from Kennedy was delayed two hours. The first leg of my six-week tour of duty. Tomorrow the John Whitmer Historical Association will meet in Springfield, where I will talk on "Joseph Smith and Abraham Lincoln." The next day, Deseret Book will sponsor a book signing between conference sessions with three television interviews scattered before and after. From then on the events come along pretty steadily until

Thanksgiving. I have a half dozen talks of various sorts ready to roll and will plug them in as seems suitable to the occasion. If they don't work on the first try, I will tighten them up and try again or discard them. I have an old talk on "Translation" left over from previous firesides, the Claremont talk on creating the sacred, the "Many Lives" talk for Princeton, the Joseph Smith and New England talk for the Massachusetts Historical Society, the "Inner Joseph Smith" talk from the Mormon History Association meetings last year, "Joseph and Abraham" for the John Whitmer Historical Association meetings in Springfield, Illinois, and now the Book of Mormon paper for the Charles Warren Center.

A few strokes today. The best was from David Armitage, the brilliant intellectual historian who left Columbia to take a job at Harvard. We were together to examine a student defending his dissertation. At the end, David said he would be coming to the Charles Warren Center seminar where I perform a week from tomorrow. He said he had read the paper on how to deal with the Book of Mormon which was distributed in advance. He thought it "spectacular." He leans toward extravagant praise, but he said it with some enthusiasm. That warmed my heart because I never know if I am getting through to my various audiences. We shall see in the event. Also notes from Jerry Bradford at ISPART and my son Karl Bushman, both happy with the book. Karl said it is a page-turner, music to my ears since I tried to make it readable and interesting.

October 1, 2005

3:38 a.m. Sitting in the Day's Inn across the street from Lambert International Airport in St. Louis. Drove back from Springfield late last night. Took me forty-five minutes, less than half the time allowed for on MapQuest. Avis people upgraded me from an economy car to an SUV. Told them

I would prefer something smaller. It's against my principles to drive gas guzzlers. Nothing else around but a tiny, tiny car, the rental clerk said, something I wouldn't even fit into. Loved driving the SUV. Smooth sailing at eighty miles an hour.

The John Whitmer Historical Association meetings were held in the Renaissance Hotel in downtown Springfield, an uneven place, quaint on a few streets, ragged on others. Like so many other small towns, looks like they have struggled to make the downtown work. Okay, but not glorious. State capitol, but not much of a campus for state buildings. Great capitol building itself sits on a large green plot, but other state buildings miscellaneous and scattered with no evidence of a plan. Got there in time to hear a couple of papers; then into lunch and the author-meets-the-critics session. At the last minute, they substituted Roger Launius for William Sutton. Launius is chair of space history for the Smithsonian Institution and a critic of Joseph Smith from a Community of Christ background. He sees few redeeming features in the Prophet. Ronald Numbers is a lapsed Seventh-day Adventist who does medical history at the University of Wisconsin. Also on the panel were Mark Scherer, historian for the Community of Christ, and Jana Riess, religion editor for *Publisher's Weekly*, a convert from her student years, and a very intelligent person.

The panelists in turn addressed four questions: the strongest features of *Rough Stone Rolling*, differences from other biographies, what the book fails to deal with, and has your opinion of Joseph Smith changed. After each round, I responded. Newell Bringhurst, a lapsed Mormon but friendly guy, presided. I was expecting a roast, but not so bad. By dividing the panelists' comments into four parts, none of them could develop a damning litany of failings. The most important thing in such a situation is for the author to maintain his composure, which I did. I got a few laughs every time I responded. The majority of the panelists thought that this is a great book for Latter-day Saints. Launius rather generously said that in the overall Joseph Smith historiography, this book provides a balance for Brodie and Hill—an insider's perspective. The one question I muffed was who did I write the book for. I said for New York Jews, when the real answer is for curious and open-minded general readers who want to know Joseph Smith. Those with fixed opinions already won't change their minds, but those who want to know more about Joseph will be informed. Later in the afternoon, I gave my Joseph Smith and Abraham Lincoln paper. It turned out to be too wordy at the end, so I was dropping out big chunks without any particular plan. At the end, Jan Shipps asked what I had learned about Joseph Smith I had not know before, and Robert Flanders what I had learned about America I had not known before. They were on-target questions that were, in a way, critiques. They were implicitly saying, Your experiment in comparisons did not yield fruit. What have you learned? I gave paltry answers; but even if I could not put my finger on it, I think the exercise is worthwhile. It is like traveling; the overall experience teaches you more than can be summed up in a short answer.

4:05 a.m. Time to shower and turn in the car. Flight for Salt Lake City leaves at 7:00 a.m. A television interview scheduled for 10:30 a.m. and a book signing at noon.

10:00 p.m. Sitting in my sister Cherry Silver's bedroom at the end of the day. She and Barnard picked me up at the Salt Lake airport and took me to Karen and David Davidson's apartment where I borrowed their car. I had a round of appointments until 2 p.m. and did not want to tie Cherry and Barnard up all that time. I drove the Davidsons' car to KUED on the University of Utah campus just below the Medical Center. The door was locked and I cooled my heels for twenty minutes. Wandering around outside I discovered some loungers in front. Turned out they were the filming crew watching for me to come in the back door. Ted Capener was sitting in the studio when I arrived. TV sets are always disillusioning. The studio was a big, unadorned black box with a smallish set on one side consisting mainly of two chairs and a table. The table was a rough number since the table top itself never appears on camera. Capener does a show called *Civic Dialogue.* He reminded me of Charles Osgood in his energy and good humor. We talked casually for a few minutes while the crew was setting up. He had been reading the book for the last few weeks, he said, and had three pages of questions. The pace was terrific. He made an inquiry, and after my answer he was off to something else. I liked his personal style and felt like I did okay. I had something to say on every point and did not stumble and wander about. Occasionally a good phrase would pop into my mouth. The show airs at 5:30 p.m., October 2.

After the interview, I headed directly to ZCMI. As I was getting out of the car in the parking lot, I met two young guys carrying boxes. One of them I recognized from the Joseph Smith Papers research team. It turns out they were bringing in a load of books for signing. One of their fathers was giving a copy to each of his twelve children. By the time I got to my signing station in the hall outside Deseret Book, there was a line of fifteen or twenty people waiting for a signed book. Many bought two and some as many as six or seven. They saw it as a good gift for their kids. About half the time, I signed only my name, but if asked would inscribe it to a person. Then I slapped on a label saying autographed, and the buyers went off to the cashier. My hand did not get tired as I feared, and I was not so rushed that I could not have tiny conversations. A number of old friends turned up, some from way back.

The big rush was over a little after 12:30, giving me a chance to observe the scene. Conference visitors kept walking by, and I wondered to myself, Why are they not stopping to buy? Don't they know the book of the century is here waiting for them to purchase? Deseret Book had a carton or two of books awaiting my signature. In between people, I signed those copies. By 1:30 the crowd had thinned. People were rushing off to get their Conference Center seats. Cory Maxwell, the Deseret Book official overseeing the operation, said it was okay to go. I was reluctant because the signing had been advertised as lasting until two, but I took him at his word. One of the purchasers who had introduced himself as Clayton Williams said he had an art gallery in the Eagle Gate Plaza adjoining the ZCMI Mall. On my way out, I stumbled on the gallery more or less by accident. He was showing me around when a woman came in who turned out to be a book purchaser who had come down to catch me before I left at 2:00. I told her to purchase her books and bring them back for signing. She came back and so did Dick Lambert, an old Cambridge friend, whom she had stumbled across in the store. Dick, it turned out, is on the Mormon Historic Sites board that is sponsoring the placement of the Joseph Smith statue in New York. We talked shop for a while with Clayton Williams joining in from time to time. It was a strange little eddy in the day. I got back to Cherry's in time for the last hour of conference.

October 2, 2005

7:00 p.m. I awoke feeling anxious, a strange reaction after a generally lovely day. I was thinking of Laura Sumsion's plans for a second Deseret Book signing. Earlier Deseret Book said they wanted to schedule a large evening reception in the Joseph Smith Memorial Building. I built my schedule in late October around that event. Yesterday she said they would have a noon book signing in the hall outside their store. Ah, I said to myself, the pullback is beginning. That messes up my schedule a little but nothing major. Having foreseen a slight retreat, I was not surprised and really not disappointed. Having a reception in the Joseph Smith Memorial Building comes too close to an official endorsement, something the Church cannot and should not give.

That little worry was overshadowed by my concern about my Massachusetts Historical Society talk next week. I know it is too long. I wondered if it is too gangly. Does it cohere? I got up thinking I would cut out a portion on the Book of Mormon as an anti-nationalist narrative. But sitting up in bed, I thought again and began to see how to strengthen that argument. I had brought the talk with me on a flash drive and for the past two hours have been revising to incorporate my new thinking. Now I see the analysis of the Book of Mormon as one of the most interesting parts of the talk. In fact I have even thought of carrying over this part to my comments at the Harvard seminar the next day. Once again I feel inspiration working through revision, by which I mean help from heaven coming in small increments which I carry out in time. I have adopted as my mantra: "Today I will be a follower of Jesus Christ." I say it over and over during the day to settle my soul. Based on experiences like this morning, I feel that it works. The words bring me into focus and close the doors on extraneous excursions that lead into silliness and frivolity on the one hand or gloom on the other. What's more I get useful ideas that seem to come from nowhere.

October 3, 2005

Last day in Utah. Today a TV interview for an early morning show, then on to Provo for an appointment with Andrew Skinner, the new head of ISPART, and another interview with the BYU TV station. In the afternoon I signed books at Benchmark for people who have already purchased the volume and then in to President Packer's office to leave a copy of the book. Tomorrow I catch an early morning plane back to New York. Yesterday after the morning session of conference, they aired the Carole Mikita show on the Prophet. It covered his life from the beginning down to his present-day reputation. Carole is a terrific reporter, businesslike, direct, fast-paced.

She had taped an interview with me last August, and I appeared as a talking head three or four times very briefly. Actually, I was not so much a talking head as a talking prune. Something about the lighting emphasized the furrows in my brow and the deep smile lines in my face. What a pitiful sight. After watching two sessions of conference, I realized how far out on the edge of things I and my little book are. One tiny stroke in the whole picture.

October 4, 2005

A good day at Brigham Young University yesterday. The most important occurrence was Andy Skinner's agreement to sponsor the Joseph Smith Summer Seminar next year. We have the money and only needed an institutional home. He agreed to provide secretarial support and handle applications and finances. The seminars are an easy sell because they have been so successful. For seven years, LDS students from all over the country have come to Provo for eight weeks to work on the cultural environment of Joseph Smith (save for one summer when they studied Latter-day Saint women in the twentieth century under Claudia.) Everyone agrees that the papers they produced and the energy they brought to the campus were beneficial. Perhaps most important, we have got to know them and they learn more about scholarship at BYU. The whole operation was made possible by the work of David and Karen Davidson in raising funds for the students' stipends and living allowances. The Davidsons have been the unseen benefactors of the book, too, providing a car and accommodations and pickup service at the airport whenever I came to Utah.

Andy is taking responsibility for reviving as many of the former Smith Institute programs as he can, recognizing the incongruity of a Church university with no Mormon studies. After seeing Andy, I made my way to the KBYU studios for an interview. Sarah Jane Buhr, the producer, had contacted me a month ago or so and made the appointment. Turns out that one of their disk jockeys on the predominantly classical music station has proposed a talk show modeled after Ted Capener's *Civic Dialogue* program on KUED. It is something of a risk because it will be unscripted with the chance of controversial stuff being aired. The announcer, a man named Marcus Smith, has recorded ten half-hour interviews exploring the life of the mind at BYU. Mine was the eleventh. It possibly will be aired around Joseph Smith's birthday in December. The others, if all goes well, will begin in January 2006. The show went pretty well, I thought. The half hour sped by; and with that much time, I felt free to elaborate my thoughts a little. In the morning I had a three-minute interview on Channel 13, the Fox station in Utah. It was almost nothing. On the way back from Provo I stopped at Benchmark Books to sign copies of *Rough Stone Rolling*. They had sold a number on the provision they were signed. When I was through with those, I signed more for regular stock. For some buyers this seems to make a difference. Curt agreed to sponsor another book signing in the afternoon of the day I will sign at Deseret Book, thus replacing the reception originally planned for October 27. On the way between Provo and Benchmark, I phoned Claudia. This must be dangerous because I remember virtually nothing of the road. My mind was wholly invested in our conversation. She said that Amazon had sent her an ad for *Rough Stone Rolling*, probably because she had bought a Mormon book of some kind from them. They get the goods on you once you are in their clutches. Check the rankings, she said; I was something like 193 the day before and 145 on Monday. That is truly an amazing number—doubtless boosted by people getting the ad. I wonder who the purchasers are. I imagine them being all Mormons, but there probably are others with a curiosity about Joseph Smith. What really surprises me is how many people have been aware of this book coming out or know about me. How did that happen? A surprising number of people seem to know about *Believing History*. If I had planned a publicity campaign, I could not have done better than to publish a preview book the year before. Many thanks to Jed and Reid for dreaming up that volume. I will be relieved to get out of the spotlight, but it is getting less uncomfortable. When people praise the book, I just let it roll off. I hope I can bear the criticism as well.

I am getting a little mercenary about the book sales. I keep thinking how nice it would be to pay off the two mortgages on our Provo house and maybe even have enough for a small cash reserve. The book seems to be selling pretty well on its release and should get another burst of sales for Christmas. If they could actually sell the 40,000 books in the print run, there would probably be enough royalties to meet that goal. I would like Claudia to be financially secure were I to die in the near future. Paying down the mortgages would help a lot.

October 6, 2005

I am sitting in the Whitney and Roger Johnson's family room in Southboro, Massachusetts, after dinner and a fireside at their house last night. Whitney and Laurel Ulrich invited a collection of about twenty-five graduate students and local scholars to hear me discuss Joseph Smith, along with Clayton Christiansen, the church's Area Authority and professor at the Harvard Business School. I told them about how I came to write the book and my empathetic approach. I posed the question whether a book about Joseph Smith written by a Mormon can be useful to non-Mormons. I thought, of course, it could until George Marsden said this is a biography for Mormons only, a theme repeated at the John Whitmer panel last week. Too sympathetic, bordering on the apologetic, I guess they have concluded. In my heart of hearts, I say to myself, you don't like it because you don't like Joseph Smith. You want him to be an impostor and a scoundrel; and when I make him something more, you conclude I am an apologist. The reverse side of my book not being helpful to others is that books about Joseph Smith by non-members are not useful to Mormons. It appears, we must divide the scholarship sharply in two. After the discussion last night, Clayton Christiansen asked if Mormons suffer from greater prejudice against their scholarship than others. What about books on Luther by Lutherans or on Christ by Christians? Is that work considered too partisan for anyone else? It was a question I could not answer. I secretly suspect Clayton is right. Joseph Smith is simply too far off the map for serious consideration. Anyone who tries to bring him back on the map must be a partisan.

October 7, 2005

I am a little frustrated this morning. I am sitting in the half-dark living room of a suite in the Eliot Hotel on Commonwealth Avenue and Massachusetts Avenue in Boston. Claudia is still asleep in the adjoining room, and I am working with the light slanting in from the hall and the glow from the computer screen. My frustration comes from not finding the charger for my cell phone. I thought I put it in my suitcase but must have left it on the table in the apartment. I will need it today because a man from a *Newsweek* radio talk show is calling at 6:00 p.m. for a ten-minute interview. He first called while we were looking at the Copley portraits in the Boston Museum of Fine Arts. (A fabulous collection of many famous pieces.) He said *Newsweek* is releasing the Joseph Smith cover on Monday; and as part of the package, they are covering the story in their weekly radio broadcast. He will call me on the cell at 6:00 p.m. today, and I will call him back on a land line for the ten-minute segment. It is pre-recorded so the exact timing is less crucial, but I want to be on time. My paper on the Book of Mormon will be discussed at the Charles Warren Center seminar on intellectual history beginning at 4:00 p.m., but I figure I will be through in time to slip up to the Charles Warren Center and take the call. I hope my cell does not run out of juice before he gets through. I have his studio phone number, so I can always call him directly.

The Eliot Hotel accommodations came with my talk at the Massachusetts Historical Society yesterday afternoon. They had books to sell and autograph but had many left over. About thirty people showed up, five or six of them MHS staff. In terms of numbers it was no great hit, but the talk went well. William Saltonstall, the MHS Council vice-president, introduced me with lots of references to my Mormonism. Where I was born, my Church callings, the fact that I answer questions on the BYU website. I realized afterward that having Mitt Romney as governor makes Massachusetts people aware of Mormonism more than they otherwise would be. I also came to see that they were a little nervous about my talk. Could I pull this off without being embarrassing? I think I did.

My theme was how Joseph Smith left New England and how it left him. In the end, I argued, New England came back. Mormonism was the culmination of the visionary stream in New England culture as Unitarianism was the culmination of the region's rationalism. I got a hearty round of applause and good questions at the end. The talk has more to it than I had thought. One man said it had the makings of five or six talks. Mostly it affirmed my feeling that I have found a middle-ground language for discussing Mormonism that is accessible to all parties. So far as I could tell, Karl Haglund was the only Mormon in the crowd, and I missed the chance to talk to him before he slipped out. I wonder if he thinks I abandoned the faith. I don't think so. After it was over, I wondered if the small turnout augured poorly for the Princeton Club talk. I hope enough of my Mormon friends turn up to fill a few chairs. I don't mind talking to a small group, but I don't want Leonard Milberg, the chair of the lecture series, to be embarrassed by the numbers.

The sun is rising over the Boston skyline. We have to call the valets early for our car because the Red Sox play this afternoon and the traffic will be snarled. They are down two games in the playoff series to the White Sox, and everyone wonders if they can pull off another miracle finish.

October 8, 2005

In some ways, yesterday was the biggest day of all my speaking tours this fall. Not in number of appearances but in import. I had lunch at the Harvard Divinity School with a dozen LDS students, informal and easy, and only one other engagement. But that was a seminar at the Charles Warren Center at Harvard arranged by Laurel Ulrich who is directing the center this year. The theme is American intellectual history, and a paper on the Book of Mormon fit the requirements. It was distributed electronically in advance and then discussed by the group. I gave a ten-minute introduction, and then Charles Capper, a Boston University historian in residence at the Warren Center this year, commented. I had heard from David Armitage, my former colleague at Columbia and now a professor at Harvard, that he liked the paper. Jeff Sklansky, a former Columbia graduate student and also a Warren fellow said he thought the paper did a good job. So I had premonitions that I had connected. Charles's comments were positive too; he couldn't be too harsh because we are friends from way back and served on the Bancroft Prize committee together a few years back.

We met in a kind of library-seminar room in Robinson Hall lined with book shelves. High up on the walls was one of those balconies with more books going up to the ceiling. A big square table in the center was surrounded by chairs with more chairs against the walls. The room was packed—probably fifty people or more. Various Mormons turned up but also faculty—

David Hall, an old friend, James Kloppenberg, an intellectual historian, Bernard Bailyn, my dissertation director. The first question I received was, Why not think of the Book of Mormon as a hoax? I asked in return, Why think of it as a hoax? That is a way of dismissing the text rather than dealing with it. It reflects on the character of Joseph Smith but says nothing about the nature of the book. The discussion moved pretty well from there. Lots of people raised their hands and made comments.

At one point a man in a suit with a black name tag on his pocket said, Why not admit that this book was beyond the capacity of Joseph Smith to write himself? To relieve the tension, I told the group the black tag identified the young man as missionary—and got a laugh. I hope he did not feel put down. Pauline Maier, an old friend and faculty member at MIT, said that we should pay attention to what the missionary had said. Why not consider the possibility that the book was inspired, and likened it to the Great Awakening. Might it not have been a work of God? I said it might be a tantalizing possibility to dangle before the class. Capper made the best response. We have to ask whether such an assertion closes down discussion or opens it up. That is the problem with talking about the inspiration of the book; it stops conversation. I was worried then that the discussion was melding into talk about modern Mormonism and our claims to truth, which would indeed close down the discussion, but we continued on in a more objective vein until about 5:45. I thought it was an okay discussion, not really scintillating. We could not seem to focus on an issue that people would return to.

David Hall asked a question that no one understood and which I did not get my mind around until the morning after. He said, If the Book of Mormon is a kind of Bible, why don't people at the Divinity School use it to understand Christ more completely? The answer seems obvious; they think it is a hoax. Why should they take it seriously? The query was baffling. Later I realized he was saying the Book of Mormon, which I say is a Bible, does not function as a Bible in the culture—which is obviously true. In what sense, then, is it a Bible? My answer now would be it functions as a Bible inside itself. If we ask what the text tells us about itself, it announces itself as a Bible. The issue is not, Why did it not work as such, but what does it ask us to do?

Later Chris Capozzolla, now teaching at MIT, said I had not convinced him to use the Book of Mormon in his courses. What, for example, would be the preceding and succeeding readings? I said Thomas Paine's *Age of Reason*, as a starter, but then went on to say the problem is not in the book, but in our understanding of the period. The Book of Mormon calls upon us to ask how was the Bible being dealt with in this period. What were the strains on this iconic text? The Book of Mormon is in conversation with those issues. It requires us to find the texts that give the book meaning. We have to look again at our intellectual history. Are we dealing adequately with the treatment of the Bible in our culture? If we cannot find the context for the Book of Mormon, perhaps we don't understand the period.

One other exchange was profitable from my point of view. One of Laurel's students, a woman working on Native Americans and probably one herself, asked about Native American prophecies in this era. They tell an entirely different story than the Book of Mormon. How do we reconcile the two? I don't think I caught the drift of her question, since it seemed to assume both texts were inspired and the question was, Why did inspired texts yield conflicting answers? We went back and forth a couple of times, until finally I said that we needed a broader look at speculations about Indian origins to provide a proper context for the Book of Mormon. At my instigation, Jared Hickman, an LDS graduate student, had earlier said that the absence of the Indians had heightened reflections on the pathos of the vanishing Americans. I acknowledged the value of gathering all of these speculations together and setting the Book of Mormon in this scene.

Laurel invited us to her house for dinner afterward and more discussion. While she and Gale drove us home she asked what I thought of the discussion. I said I thought it had its ups and downs, and she went on to report rave reviews. I can't believe everyone felt that way, but then she said that just discussing the Book of Mormon in that context was a breakthrough. I suppose it was a historic occasion like the symposium on Joseph Smith at the Library of Congress. She liked the fact that I proposed a way of talking about the book while remaining perfectly orthodox. That, of course, is exactly what I wanted to do. There is a lot more work ahead, but I got us part of the way.

Jed sent me an email today with a review from the *New York Sun*. Someone must have put it on an LDS blog. They reviewer was most attracted to my chapter on the Book of Mormon. He thought I laid out the issues very well. It's the most gratifying review thus far. He spots me as a believer and comments on my refusal to use the word "alleged" before every revelation, and still was not put off. The comparison was to Robert Remini's biography of Joseph, a book mentioned in an earlier review. He said Remini did a terrific job of setting Joseph in the context of the Second Great Awakening. I suppose I could have sketched in those connections, but I thought of them as fairly superficial and focused instead on the visionary culture. I forget how people like a subject connected to the familiar. You help them by simply using a familiar term.

The reviewer concludes by writing:

> More than that, "The Book of Mormon" has a universalist message; the "American story does not control the narrative," Mr. Bushman writes. It does not celebrate democ-

racy, the biographer insists, but "endlessly expounds the master biblical narrative—the history of Israel." The text proposes, in Mr. Bushman's words, "a new purpose for America: becoming a realm of righteousness rather than an empire of liberty."

If I have focused on Mr. Bushman's interpretation of "The Book of Mormon," it is because he brings his discussion back to biography—its power and its limitations:

Biographical analysis runs the risk of making creative works little more than a mirror of the author's life. As one critic puts it, "The book is far grander, much broader, and its internal logic and power go well beyond the life of Joseph Smith." By delineating the boundaries of biography so sensitively, Mr. Bushman has paradoxically enhanced its authority.

On top of a positive review, I feel pretty good all in all about the Harvard event. I kept my composure and made a room full of people take the Book of Mormon seriously for a few minutes. I didn't abandon either portion of my identity; I was always the historian and always the Mormon. Jared Hickman does it better than I do, but he borders on the unorthodox and doesn't always carry believers along with him. I take fewer risks but keep the Mormons on my side.

October 9, 2005

Sitting in the Sturbridge Coach Inn early Sunday morning. When Claudia and I returned from speaking to the singles conference at the Harvard Business School, we found we had been ejected from the room the Charles Warren Center had provided. The center paid for only one night, not two. I had misread the reservation card and thought they had generously covered both nights. Instead the clerks had cleaned out our room and made space for someone else. As it turned out, it was all for the good. We left for New York after talking at Weston—twenty miles from Boston in the New York direction. It was raining furiously, so we stopped at a motel in Sturbridge, a quarter of the way home.

About six hundred kids showed up for the singles conference sponsored by the Cambridge Stake. More people come from a distance than enroll from the local area. The local students have higher priorities, it seems. Claudia spoke first on "Presenting Joseph Smith," reviewing the various ways she and the Church have presented the Prophet. I spoke on "Joseph Smith for Strivers." As it turned out, the talk went over well. It was designed for students and went down with them. I was pleased because it means I can give the same talk at the Stanford convocation in two weeks. The Weston talk was a repeat of the Mormon History Association address on "The Inner Joseph Smith." Whitney Johnson had loved that talk and urged me to give it again. I think it was okay. People listened, but it gives too much new material for a standard LDS audience. I think the listeners were a little stunned. I am glad I floated this balloon here, because I now know to try something else in Kansas City. The talk for the singles seems like a better choice.

October 10, 2005

The *Newsweek* article on Joseph Smith is due out today. Eric Mason, a student in the NEH summer seminar, circulated news that it was online last night. I was amazed to see that Elise Soukup got the byline, meaning that Jon Meacham, the chief editor who does the religion stories, did not change her draft very much. It was as sympathetic a portrait of the prophet as we could expect. I got quoted a few times and the book was mentioned. We are getting somewhere when a Latter-day Saint writes the article on Joseph Smith for *Newsweek*.

Richard Lyman Bushman

I am beginning to get letters from people who have problems with aspects of Joseph Smith's life. One from a Mormon professor asked about polyandry and Joseph's marriages to young girls. I am not able to quiet all their apprehensions but say what I can. We have to live with perplexities. Here is my attempted answer.

> I can't really make sense of all you refer to. The marriage to the fourteen-year-old doesn't bother me so much because young girls were frequently married at that age in those days. Joseph was binding all sorts of people to him, including women in their fifties. The marriage could be as readily interpreted as an offer of protection as exploitation of a young girl. Polyandry shakes up lots of our people. It seems incongruous with our view of companionate marriage today. You might say that for a woman to have more than one husband is no more shocking than for a man to have more than one wife, but what about the poor first husband? He was too often left out in the cold. It seems as if Joseph wanted to bind everyone to everyone else without regard to personal bonds. That is hard for us to understand these days.
>
> Richard

October 13, 2005

I neglected to write about my Princeton Club talk yesterday. It was one of those addresses that went far better than anticipated. The morning of the talk I felt there were some soggy parts, especially near the end. I chewed them over for a while, asking the question, What will be interesting and helpful to the audience? and on that basis strengthened the argument. (I see this process of improvement everywhere I turn these days.) The audience seemed to be fairly enthusiastic about the results—Mormon and non-Mormons alike. I had made a little effort to be sure people in the New York Stake knew about the talk and they turned out in fair numbers. They had to bring in extra chairs for people in the back. Elise Soukup, author of the *Newsweek* article on Mormons was there with her husband. The attendance pleased me. I knew the topic would not attract a big crowd of non-Mormons, and I did not want Leonard Milberg, chair of the library committee, to be embarrassed. I think he was happy with the occasion. While preparing the talk, it occurred to me to recognize his achievements in leading the library committee for many years. I think he was genuinely pleased; he came up and hugged me afterwards. The most interesting reaction was Claudia's comment that the talk got stronger as it went along.

In her mind, the soggy last section was the best part. She also thought my answers to questions were a "triumph." I certainly did not get that impression myself. I simply said something in response. I think she is impressed that I have facts to support my statements, but I have been laboring away on Joseph Smith for eight years now. The real triumph was the tone. I can now speak in a way that reaches non-Mormons while not offending Mormons. It makes them happy for me to be relaxed—to be able to bring out negative matters without destroying the prophet, and at the same time to make his achievements admirable.

Fan mail:

Dear Brother Bushman,

Just a quick note to tell you how much I appreciated your wonderful book on Joseph. I love biographies and read them often. I cannot think of a biography that I have enjoyed more than this one. The scholarship, the sensitivity to doctrinal truths, the determination to present an honest and straightforward history, all combined for a wonderful read. I feel like I understand the prophet better than I ever have before, and I come away beaming with pride thinking about of my religious heritage. I am very excited about the terrific quality of scholarship devoted to this topic by one of our own faith. I expected this to be a wonderful book and was surprised in so many ways with the richness of the interpretations and the excitement of the story told. I look forward to reading it again.

Thanks!

Steve Hood
Ursinus College

October 14, 2005

This review turned up on the Amazon page for *Rough Stone Rolling*:

Certainly one of the most difficult of biographical projects is to undertake a controversial religious figure like Joseph Smith. Until this book, Joseph Smith biographies have either been hagiographies or have treated Smith as a charismatic charlatan. The hagiographies are of little interest to those seeking a reasonably objective and scholarly account. However, the books treating Smith as a charismatic charlatan fail as well, for they offer no understanding of how Smith succeeded in setting up a religion which not only survived but thrived after he was dead. And it is this which makes Smith worth studying. There are more interesting characters than Smith to study if one's interest is just debunking a charlatan. It is how Smith succeeded at what Harold Bloom calls "religion-making" that sets Smith apart. And it is here where Bushman exceeds any other Smith biography—indeed attempts what no other Smith biography attempts. This is to try to understand Joseph Smith as a creator of a new religious worldview. Of course, all of the controversial matters are covered fairly and as completely as space allows in a one-volume work. However, this biography also for the first time gives us a realistic portrait of a very human and flawed man who nonetheless behaved as though he was driven by a holy vision, a vision of a saintly commonwealth both in the heavens and on earth—a vision which engaged thousands of his contemporaries and continues to engage millions today.

That is exactly the kind of reader I had hoped for. I would like to think it is written by a non-Mormon, a curious general reader who does not think Joseph was necessarily a scoundrel. On the Mormon side, Alan Jacobsen, a temple missionary here for a few months, wrote to say he likes the book too. That is a pretty good range, since I think of the Jacobsens as fairly conservative. High conservatives may not like it, and determined Joseph Smith skeptics won't either. But there is a good-sized group in between. Hurrah!

I look up my Amazon rank a couple of times a day. I tell myself I am curious about how the system works, but it is mainly vanity I know. They rank books by sales that day and the day before. My guess is that they base it on sales for the past twenty-four hours and the twenty-four before that, so the number keeps changing through the day. In the past week, I have been in the two hundreds, with a couple of days in the one hundreds. Incredible numbers for the subject and for me. Shows that Mormons are passing the word around.

October 18, 2005

Not much happening on the book front. The Amazon rankings remain in the 200s, a marvel. I keep expecting them to drop as the novelty wears off. Not so far. The rank usually improves on Mondays, a result, I am guessing, from word passed along at church. I get compliments from Latter-day Saints, and one laudatory note from Lillian Handlin who is reading the copy we gave to her and Oscar, my teacher at Harvard. Right now I am feeling more or less indifferent to reactions; that doubtless will change when hard-hitting reviews turn up in newspapers—or they fail to review it at all. I feel that I have a solid audience thus far. The distance between me and my brain child is probably widening. I am more concerned about all the talks I have to give. The talk in Kansas City at my son's stake was a little off key. Serge's wife Patty had arranged for the engagement at a big Relief Society event. For some reason, the talk was not exactly on target. I am trying to tune it up for Stanford and Orange County this week. I call it "The Life and Teachings of Joseph Smith," and try to draw out lessons for our lives. Rather than abandoning talks when they fall flat, I am following my improvement-in-time technique. I tweak them here and there to sharpen the argument.

October 24, 2005

Back from the wars. Just completed a circuit from Palo Alto to Claremont to Orange County to New York City talking to Mormons and mixed audiences. All the talks met the requirements from what I could tell. Those who came forward afterward to have me sign books or chat were appropriately pleased, leaving me with no regrets. I think I have a collection of talks that fill the bill pretty well. After some of the talks, I fielded questions, perhaps the most interesting part of the evening, according to Claudia who attended the fireside in the New York Stake. People like to bring up their most difficult questions and feel that they get a straight answer based on real evidence. She suggested an evening devoted entirely to questions. Along the way I met lots of old friends and new and interesting people.

I am getting lots of evidence that the Mormons like the book. People speak of buying it in numbers to give to their children and friends. Comments are good, some wildly extravagant. One from an enthusiastic trainer of secondary school teachers whom I helped out one summer in a workshop with history honors teachers compared it to Beethoven's "Ode to Joy." That's one I should pass along to Knopf.

I came home half thinking I would have the *Times* review to face this Sunday—but nothing. Now it is dawning on me the *Times* may not review the book. It may seem too parochial for their audience. Not a loss, really. The readership is going to be heavily Mormon, and they don't need the *Times* to learn about the book. I was worried about embarrassing my Mormon fans anyway. They would be disappointed to see me taken apart in public by a *Times* reviewer. Neglect may be the best course. So far none of the big newspapers have dealt with the book. The *New York Sun*, in fact, is the only newspaper review to date. Knopf sends reviews as they come along, so I should see whatever appears.

October 26, 2005

Shreveport, Louisiana. Clear sky, slightly nippy weather. Conference on Joseph Smith at Centenary College, a Methodist-related school with a religious studies department. Peter Huff, chair, led seven students on a tour of Mormon sites this past summer and is following up with five evening programs on Joseph Smith. Jan Shipps, Bob Millet, and I are speaking, and the Monday and Friday evenings are Joseph Smith films, *American Prophet* and *Legacy*. I gather it's a conservative town, strongly Baptist with a scattering of Catholics. Last night after her presentation, Jan got the classic question about adding to the Bible contrary to the passage warning about so doing. I am going to give the same talk I gave to the heavily Jewish audience at the Princeton Club. This morning I read it over with the Shreveport audience in mind. I sense possible pitfalls but can't quite identify what they are. I will keep thinking through the day and adjust in the afternoon before the talk—if inspiration strikes. I am as likely to offend the Mormons in the audience as the evangelicals. Jan got tripped up because she said a prophet must have believers before he is truly a prophet. A Mormon in the audience objected. They want the gospel straight with no fancy philosophical interpretations. I may be snared in the same trap. Copies of my book were on sale but few of them sold. I realize a new biography of JS does not register with many Saints. They know his life; why read 500 pages to learn what they already know?

October 28, 2005 - I

Two book signings in Salt Lake City yesterday—noon at Deseret Book and 5:00 p.m. at Benchmark. An AP reporter named Jennifer Dobner interviewed me at Deseret Book for an AP wire service article she is writing. Many complimentary comments from people who were reading the book. One man said I was raised up in this generation to write the book. He hit a soft spot, and I nearly broke into tears. Later at Benchmark, a heavily male clientele filled the room and spilled out into the hall. I gave a short spiel about my approach in writing the book and then fielded questions.

Some difficult or tough questions, one by a physicist who questioned my use of Ptolemaic and Copernican astronomies in the chapter on Abraham; Bob Vernon raised the Book of Abraham translation problems; Will Bagley, the old gadfly, asked about a book he called Joseph Jackson's *Tales of Old Nauvoo* (turned out he had the title wrong, it's *A Narrative of the Adventures and Experiences of Joseph H. Jackson in Nauvoo: Disclosing the Depths of Mormon Villainy* [1844]). Not too graceful in the answers. I got nervous under the physicist's fire, admitting I did not know too much about astronomy and that the Abraham schemes don't conform to any standard astronomy. I gave my standard take on Abraham: There are problems with the translation but the contents of the book are strikingly like other apocryphal Abraham texts. To Bagley I had to admit I had not seen the Jackson book and did not even know about it. Embarrassing, and I said so. Bagley said that Jackson presents a persuasive psychology of Joseph, going from one sexual exploit to another in crescendo, culminating in plural marriage. Apparently much in the John C. Bennett spirit. I said that Joseph had always been suspicious of Jackson since he got to Nauvoo and would not be confessing his sins to him. He feared Jackson was after his life. I said that I was suspicious of many charges against Joseph, especially if written much later. Bagley retorted that it was published in 1844. I was a little ruffled, though I recovered well enough after. Today I have to go down early to the Church History Department library to hunt down this book. I can't understand why I would not have run across this volume before, not even a reference that I can remember. My guess in advance, especially if being written in 1844, is that it was an attempt to discredit JS by the apostate faction in Nauvoo, and to raise the countryside against him. I am writing now at 1:30 a.m. after awakening with a troubled heart. I don't like to be caught off base like that. I will ask Dean Jessee and Mark Ashurst-McGee what they think of the book. [I looked at the book the next day and found it to be in the category of John C. Bennett's *The History of the Saints*. Possibly some truth there but lots of exaggeration.]

My son Ben came to the signing after finishing his work in Draper where his small computer firm has an office. Afterwards we had dinner at a nearby Chinese restaurant. He was curious about my answer to a question about any inspiration I had while writing the book. The questioner wanted to know if any doctrines had come to me strongly. I replied that some had, but I could not say much about them in that setting. Ben was intrigued by my mysterious evasion, and I told him that some of the doctrines I considered most valuable to my inner life were incommunicable. When I tried, they fell flat. Later in the discussion, he said he was working with the idea that God had optimized the world to the maximum benefit of all his children. I replied this implied he actually controlled everything, leaving us with no free agency. We went back and forth on this point rather unsatisfactorily. I could not make myself clear, underscoring my feeling about my favorite doctrines going nowhere when I try to describe them. My reservations go beyond my inability to describe them to my uncertainty about their validity. Am I demeaning God in not allowing him perfect control over all events and perfect knowledge of everything that will happen? What is my point of view?

1. God is one of a number of superior intelligences who have learned—how we do not know exactly—to obtain glory and intelligence. They can create worlds and do much else.

2. These gods take us lesser intelligences, swimming about like fish in the sea, under their tutelage, saying they will teach us how to achieve intelligence and glory.

3. One of their great lessons is that we can do more acting together than we can standing (or swimming) alone. Thus, they bind us to them with multiple covenants.

4. We are not only to obey them; we are to join with our brothers and sisters in the order of the priesthood under God's direction. This priesthood goes back before the foundations of the earth and includes all the gods who have gone before. They are bound into one God whose combined force and intelligence is the source of glory. We may even add to the glory by joining them—like computers strung in parallel, generating computing power. Hence the essential importance of unity.

5. In this sense, the priesthood is God. When joined together like the council of gods that organized the earth, it manifests

its godly powers. At the same time, any one God can speak for the whole because they are unified. Adam can become the God of this earth under Christ's suzerainty.

6. We exist on the ragged edges of this holy order, but in sub-scribing to it we join the grand alliance that rules the godly universe.

7. Outside of this created order, only chaos reigns, but in the outer darkness are other intelligences such as Lucifer who have orders and priesthoods of their own, independent of and possibly in opposition to Elohim's.

8. Within the created order, the intelligences find their places, some as animals, some as stones perhaps, some as humans. The diversity of forms on the earth suggests the diversity of unorganized intelligences. Hence the detail in the temple account of creation of the many forms of life, each to fulfill the measure of its creation.

9. Ben believes each of these intelligences will assuredly find its true place where it can maximize its possibility. God will guarantee that. He may be right, but I suggested the alternative view that God is constantly recruiting intelli-gences to the godly path and the success of this operation depends on us. If we attract people to Christ, they get included; if someone doesn't reach them, these souls may slip to a lesser spot. God will not necessarily guarantee everyone the highest possible position for his or her intelli-gence. Some may fall to a lower rung because there was no one there to raise them up. It is scary, but it makes life real. What makes it less scary is that there are many ways to grow in intelligence. The Mormons are not the only source of light. Christ radiates throughout the world, through many voices. We need only to listen to one to set our foot on the right path.

As I write, this doctrine tastes good to me. I believe it is the truth. All of it can be found in Joseph's teachings. But it is not being taught by the Church today. Jennifer Dobner, the AP reporter, told me after the book signing that the Church chastised her for writing about doctrines of this kind, as if they felt they discredited the Church. President Hinckley has said he does not put much stock in such teachings. That may be the proper position for today when we are under attack from evangelical Christians. It would be a mistake, however, to discard them entirely. They are a precious cultural resource. It may be one function of my book to sustain their life by explicating Joseph's thought as part of the campaign to preserve doctrine.

October 28, 2005 - II

Another day of signings and a speech. After spending the morning at the JS Papers offices in the Church Office Building, I headed south, stopping for a half hour at Benchmark to put signatures on books they are offering for sale. Then on to the BYU Bookstore. I was ten minutes late because of parking troubles, and a line of ten or fifteen people was waiting. For two hours I signed away at a rapid pace with a line of a dozen people there most of the time. I met old friends and relatives—Betsy Goodliffe came by and one of the Wirthlin boys. I have no idea how many books they sold, but a huge stack went down. When I finally got up to leave, they were stocking a table with more copies—probably four or five dozen books. I get lots of praise—people enjoy the read, their lives are changed, this is just what they have been waiting for. The reception is far more enthusiastic than I expected. Of course, I hear only the favorable comments, but they are frequent and consistent. I seem to have satisfied one of my major audiences.

In midafternoon, I called Claudia. At the end of the conversation, she said, "I probably should not say this but you have a

review in the *New York Review of Books*, and it is negative."
Turns out Larry McMurtry, a fan of western history, did the
review. Claudia read the whole thing to me over the phone.
Actually I didn't think it was that bad. It really reviewed
Joseph Smith rather than me, and McMurtry does not think
that well of the Prophet. He is really hung up on the gold
plates and plural marriage. The only chastisement I receive is
over my refusal to face up to the plates problem. Otherwise
I am pretty much invisible in the essay. The biggest disappointment is that McMurtry did not find a thing in the book
to cause him to reconsider—or even to see a problem in—his
understanding of Joseph. My guess is that he read only the
first part of the book and the sections on plural marriage.
That is all he talked about. So while disappointed in him, I
was not depressed by the review. Actually I am pleased the
book made it into the *New York Review of Books*. I thought
they would pass it by. It increases my hope that the *Times*
will eventually review the book. I am surprised that more
newspapers haven't reviewed it yet—especially the *Los
Angeles Times* with its large Mormon readership.

How am I feeling about the book right now? Steady and
confident but not giddy. It is far more successful among
Mormons than I dared expect. I still worry that readers will
be disappointed as they read further. Mormons will be
shocked by my revelations of Joseph's character; non-
Mormons will think I am too partisan. I remain wary. At
the same time, the confidence base is firming up. Besides
good comments on the book, my talks have been going down
pretty well. I can always be tripped up I know, but recently
I seem to be in a pretty good groove. I still keep saying my
mantra about Christ over and over: "Today I will be a follower of Jesus Christ." That, as much as the good response
to the book, has settled my soul.

Tonight I spoke on Joseph Smith and Abraham Lincoln, a
repeat of my John Whitmer talk, to a huge Sperry Symposium

audience at BYU—maybe 400–500 people in the auditorium and many more in overflow halls nearby.[2] Truman Madsen spoke first, then me, and finally Susan Easton Black. At each interval, I signed books and met old friends. One more talk in Moscow, Idaho, and my longest trip will be over.

November 1, 2005

Sitting in my brother Bill's living room in Kalispell, Montana, a little over an hour's flight from Spokane. Flew over in a tiny Big Sky turboprop with just one seat on each side of the aisle. The co-pilot doubled as steward and baggage man. Bill met me at the airport and drove us up into Glacier National Park which opens up just north of the town. Clouds covered the tops of the mountains, but we could see enough to know that the cliffs rise almost straight up. We came back to their beautifully decorated house, a work of art by his wife, Pam.

The day began by Wayne McKay driving me the hour and a half from Moscow, Idaho, to Spokane. My first appointment for the day had been a book-signing at Waldenbooks in the Palouse Mall in Moscow. The manager, a Latter-day Saint woman who is married to the Idaho football coach (who had won his first game of the year two days before) had ordered thirty-five copies of the book. To my great surprise, she had sold out by 9:30 a.m. People began coming in at 9:00 a.m. when the stores in the mall were still not officially open and the walkers were about the only people around. But the buyers began coming anyway. I realized that gift-giving is a big part of this routine. People want something a little special and a signed copy qualifies. One lady bought five copies. The people were spaced widely enough that I could talk to them briefly while I signed.

During the first half hour, I was on the phone to Claudia, interrupting her whenever someone stopped by. She was reading me two reviews, one from the *Salt Lake Tribune* and the other from Knight-Ridder newspapers. They were strangely mirror images of one another. The *Tribune* writer complained the book was a bore because it said nothing new and turned a very interesting man into a dull figure. He did not explain exactly what he wanted, but it was obvious that I thought too favorably of the Prophet. The Knight-Ridder reviewer thought Joseph Smith was fabulously interesting but largely because he was such a scoundrel. He pointed to all the flaws I had found in his character. I could not decide which review I liked least. One probably understood the book but condemned it; the other did not understand the argument but liked it.

I am getting pretty indifferent to the reviews. They are pretty much what I expected. People with a preformed view of Joseph as scoundrel will object; Mormons who like Joseph Smith will take a deep breath and learn from my portrayal. Somewhere in between is my ideal curious reader who wants to understand him. What is not getting through to the unbelievers is the magnitude of Joseph's accomplishments. Few of them can see much admirable or wonderful. My talk to the Princeton Club pretty much sums up the situation. The people who think him a fraud can't get beyond that judgment to assess him as a man. I am resigned to accepting this fact of life. Meanwhile the book will make its own way in the world, satisfying most Latter-day Saints and serving as an emissary to the curious. When someone wants to know more about the Prophet, this statement is available. Those who think him a fraud can stop investigating and basically stop thinking. They don't have to know more because they know enough already.

The night before, I had spoken to the Institute that serves both the University of Idaho in Moscow and Washington State in Pullman a few miles across the state border. I was entertained by Claudia's niece Betsy and her husband Kirby Dailey, the stake president. Until recently, he dry farmed 4,000 acres of the fabulous Palouse land where the roots of the soft wheat go down six to ten feet in search of water. The talk was not one of my greatest hits. Sometimes I connect, sometimes I don't.

November 2, 2005

Home again. Got in late Tuesday afternoon after flying from Kalispell to Salt Lake City and on to New York. I am caught up in a swirl of reviews and counter-reviews. Three people have protested the Larry McMurtry review in the *New York Review of Books*: Jed, Jan Shipps, and Terryl Givens. While I was away, Jed emailed friends asking for letters to the editor protesting McMurtry's review. Jed wrote his own letter and asked Nate Oman, a thinky Latter-day Saint lawyer, to sign. He also enlisted Jan Shipps and Terryl Givens. Terryl hoped he could persuade the magazine to suspend publication, but they were too far along to pull back. Here is his letter:

> Editor
> *New York Review of Books*
> In reference to "Angel in America" by Larry McMurtry
>
> The Jesuit scholar Thomas O'Dea famously said of The Book of Mormon that it "has not been universally considered by its critics as one of those books that must be read in order to have an opinion of it." The same, apparently, is true of Richard Bushman's *Rough Stone Rolling*—at least judging by Larry McMurtry's review of Fawn Brodie and her sixty-year-old biography, masquerading as a review of Bushman's new study. It is lamentable that McMurtry nowhere seriously engages either the controversial—but undeniably complex—American prophet, or the richly nuanced study by his most important biographer of the last fifty years. The *New York Review* and its readers have been shortchanged. More disturbingly, the *Review*, by publishing McMurtry's piece, has lent legitimacy to writing that goes beyond mere self-indulgence to flirtation with slander and religious bigotry (Mormonism's capital, and by implication the LDS church,

as the realm of "capos," "goodfellas" and "darkness"?) In my own work on Mormonism in American history, I had concluded, apparently inaccurately, that writers and journalists had, by the Smoot hearings of the early 20th century, moved beyond the sensationalism and bad faith that contributed to decades of conflict, hatred, and persecution.

Responsible journalism calls for reviewers to show evidence of having read the books they purport to review. Responsible citizenship, in today's world especially, calls for editors to foster religious understanding and tolerance rather than caricature and gratuitous defamation. I hope the errors in judgment both have shown in this case will not be compounded by hard-copy publication on November 17th.

Sincerely,

Terryl Givens
Professor of Literature and Religion
University of Richmond

The letter was good for being compact and hard-hitting. Jan wrote in the same spirit.

In my email last night were the comments of two sociologists from the panel on my book at the Society for the Scientific Study of Religion conference in Rochester next week. Both object to my approach. When you add the *Tribune* review to the list, I am coming under heavy fire. I am not sure I can answer all the objections. The best I can do is explain my approach and let people take it or leave it. I am grateful to Jan, Jed, and Terryl for rallying to my side. It helps to have a few comrades in arms. Beyond the immediate fray, however, the book must fend for itself. Reviews come and go but the book can never be destroyed. It will sit on the shelf and speak to readers for many years to come.

November 7, 2005

Our plane from Buffalo last night was scheduled to leave at 7:25, and didn't get away until midnight. Claudia and I had been to Palmyra for a day-long Saturday conference on Joseph Smith sponsored by the stake and a follow-up Sunday fireside in Buffalo resulting from Doug Bunker's suggestion to his stake president, a man named Free. Because we had to get back home that evening, they cancelled Sunday School, priesthood meeting, and Relief Society in the stake and held this 1:30 meeting instead. I never know if these people get what they want out of their speakers. In Palmyra they began at 9:00 in the morning and listened non-stop (save for lunch) until 6:00 at night. They invited good people—Rick Turley, Joseph McConkie, Jerry Perkins, Sheri Dew, and Larry Porter in addition to Claudia and me—and had Maurine and Scot Proctor present their recent video on Church history the night before. But I can't imagine that the talks lived up entirely to expectations. I feel the same way about the academic conferences on the Prophet. They never live up to expectations, however glorious in conception. At Palmyra, I spoke on the translation of the Book of Mormon, one of my stalwart talks, and in Buffalo I gave my talk on the life and teachings of Joseph Smith coming out of the Stanford convocation and the Boston single adults conference. Neither talk really rang the bell. Perhaps the talks tire me. I begin to see weak points in the argument or to imagine objections. Today, on the day after their delivery, I think I am going to retire both. The other alternative is to think them both through afresh but at the moment, it hardly seems worth it.

In general the euphoria of the first weeks after publication launch is fading. People still say they enjoy the book and sales are holding up reasonably well (in the high 400s on the Amazon.com list). But I no longer feel I am ushered around the country in a flood of enthusiasm. My talks are no more than okay, and the negative reviews are turning up. This morning I saw copies of letters to the editor objecting to the *Salt Lake*

Tribune review. People rush to my defense when the negatives are published. But the fact is readers will now realize that this book is not greeted everywhere with unalloyed enthusiasm. Some Mormon readers may believe its scholarship and candor will carry all before it. That is not true and probably impossible. I feel less chagrined myself by the negative reviews than unhappy about how Mormon readers will feel. The truth is they must learn the facts of life. Mormonism will not win over every honest soul who examines Joseph's record. Resistance is not always due to ignorance. The world is filled with people who think Joseph Smith is unbelievable. They must live with that fact as I do every minute of the day. Many Mormons, especially those deep in the heartland, may entertain the illusion that the truth of their religion is obvious. They will be puzzled and disillusioned by the criticism.

Last Saturday, Armand Mauss picked me up at the Palmyra Stake center and drove me to Rochester for the meetings of the Society for the Scientific Study of Religion where there was a session on my book. The Mormon branch of the society, which usually sponsors a couple of sessions, had asked four Mormon sociologists in various stages of disaffection from their Mormon pasts to comment: twin brothers Gordon and Gary Shepherd, Ryan Cragun, and Rick Phillips. All were rather generous in their comments on the book, noting its strengths before going to its weaknesses. I had asked that they discuss the question of how to write a sociological biography, and they all did pretty much. In the sociological spirit, Ryan Cragun insisted I should provide naturalistic explanations for the visionary phenomenon. The others discussed the merits of naturalism but left room for other approaches, including mine. My reply—not all that cogent—argued for an empathetic approach in the manner of Robert Orsi as opposed to Stephen Prothero. I said that it was unlikely that I could ever write a biography acceptable to all possible audiences. Because I am a Mormon, I am suspect. Empathy will be read as sympathy and ultimately as advocacy. Robert Orsi might succeed where I fall short. People might ask him to pass judgment at the end on Mormon errors and Joseph's deceptions, but they would go along with him through the empathetic parts, and Mormons would accept him as they have Jan Shipps. Possibly some non-Mormon writer could accomplish what I have attempted. I also said that I recognized one limitation in my mental makeup. Because I am a believer, I am not driven to find naturalistic explanations for Joseph's emergence as a prophet. How did he change from a rural visionary to the founder of a religion and a major spokesman for God? I recognize the importance of the question, and I am theoretically willing to consider theory-based explanations. In the early chapters, I try to map out the stages of his growth as at least a step in the direction of explanation. But in my heart of hearts, I don't feel the need to come up with something. I am quite willing to leave a hint of mystery and wonder in the process.

November 9, 2005

I wrote to Jane Garrett, my friendly editor at Knopf, that I thought people came to Joseph Smith with preconceptions they cannot let go of. Hence the McMurtry review on Joseph the gold-digger rather than the Joseph of my biography. She wrote back:

> I am very pleased that Mormons like the book. They should; it's a super book. I suppose you are right about many people coming to it with preconceptions that they resist giving up. I like to think that anyone who has had spiritual experiences themselves could recognize the importance of Joseph's experiences. Maybe some can't make that leap and maybe many have not had spiritual experiences or have not recognized them.

> All the best,

> Jane

You can see why people write books for her. She ministers to her authors' souls. I must stop being defensive about the McMurtry review. At the Princeton Library dinner on Monday, I was explaining my take on the review to Byron Hollingshead. As I got deeper into it, I realized I should not be defensive. The best defense is to remain unfazed.

The Mormon blogs have been talking about the book. I agreed to respond to reviews at Times and Seasons, and, not to be outdone, Millennial Star approached Jed for an online interview. Jed asked me to answer thirteen questions. Here they are with my answers.

Questions for Richard on *RSR* (Oct. 26, 2005)

1. *You say in the preface that* RSR *pays more attention to Joseph Smith's religious thought than previous biographies. Was there some aspect of his thought that you ended up falling in love with much to your delight? Did any aspect repel you?*

Plural marriage is hard for anyone who is happily married to understand, but it does not repel me as it does many Latter-day Saints. I can picture saintly people forming a communal bond within a household or series of households. Plural marriage drops barriers that hedge up our strongest passions, and so strikes fear into our hearts. On the appreciation side, I love the King Follett doctrines about a vastly intelligent and powerful God taking wandering, primitive spirits under his wing and teaching them how to achieve glory.

2. *What about Joseph Smith so charmed his followers? You make the point that most converts never knew the Prophet before they converted. What kept them believing after they met him?*

I don't think a lot of the Nauvoo Saints knew him intimately. They heard him speak and saw him around town but were not his intimates. Yet they did love him as you say. I think it was because he wore his heart on his sleeve. He let his anger rip and he overflowed with love. His impetuosity sometimes made him hard to live with, but people knew where they stood. A great emotionally charged personality can be magnetic.

3. *One school of thought says historians do better when they aggressively argue for a position on issues of controversy. Yet on many of the modern controversies surrounding Joseph Smith-Book of Mormon historicity, the date of Melchizedek Priesthood restoration, the place of Church organization, the meaning of polyandry—you present the evidence without coming down definitively one way or another. Why is that?*

I see no reason to solve problems that cannot be solved. When you go beyond the evidence, you get in trouble. Premature closure leads to error.

4. *You have called your historical method broadly empathetic. Did empathizing with Joseph ever make it difficult for you to empathize with Emma?*

Not in the least. I see their relationship as tragic. She believed in him but could not bear plural marriage. He loved her but could not resist his own revelation. They were both heroic actors on a large stage trapped in terrible moral dilemmas.

5. *Mormonism as a violent religion is one of the most enduring images in the popular press, starting with E. D. Howe and coming down to the present in Jon Krakauer. RSR, however, says Mormon militarism was reactive, not native to the tradition. "What could the Mormons do but*

defend themselves like a nation?" you ask rhetorically at one point (235-36). Given the perception of militarism, has Mormonism been radically misunderstood? Is it important for Joseph Smith to be known as a peace-loving prophet?

I am not sure Joseph was a peace-loving prophet. He was outraged at the treatment his people received and was passionate to overcome his enemies. He also was desperate because he could not see how to accomplish it. He brought together military bodies in Zion's Camp and the Nauvoo Legion, but he knew that resistance was futile. The Mormons would always lose in an outright war. He struggled to erect political institutions like the municipal court to protect himself and the Saints, but they were frail reeds. His failure to solve the problem of American violence was dramatically demonstrated by his death. Unfortunately, along the way he sometimes cultivated the violent elements among his followers who did wish to use force, and they were responsible for the greatest mistake in our history.

6. For a long time observers represented Joseph Smith's Mormonism as authoritarian religion. More recently, scholars like Nathan Hatch have emphasized its democratic elements. What does Joseph Smith stand to gain in this debate? What does he stand to lose?

I have chastised Nathan Hatch for leaving Christ out of *The Democratization of American Christianity.* Evangelical Christians were not setting about to be democrats, but to preach Christ crucified. He acknowledged the lacuna but justified his work on the grounds that it made Christianity more attractive in the modern world. I don't think we want to play that game. I think we are perfectly justified in claiming that Joseph Smith's teachings were radically democratic in some respects but thoroughly hierarchical in others. Both sides have to be stressed. The double-sidedness has to be kept in mind to understand the conflicts that arose when an Oliver Cowdery or a John Corrill switched from Kingdom language to republican speech. By going from one language to the other, the Kingdom virtues of obedience and consecration of properties are transformed into aspects of tyranny.

7. Joseph Smith was a man who sought to imitate the Bible. Is there anything extra-biblical about him?

"Imitate" is not exactly the word I would use. He certainly drew upon the Bible and justified virtually every doctrine with a biblical passage. The question here is, Which Bible? The Bible scarcely exists apart from interpretation. It is infinitely malleable. There is a Calvinist Bible, a Catholic Bible, scores of other Bibles, and then Joseph Smith's Bible. His originality lay not so much in going beyond the Bible but in going beyond the Protestant Bible. Priesthood, temples, corporeal God, human divinization, are all in the Bible but not the Bible Joseph's Protestant neighbors were reading. They would consider him radically extra-biblical as evangelists do today; he would think otherwise, and in some striking instances such as God working in councils, modern biblical scholarship supports Joseph Smith.

8. Is Joseph Smith an American tragedy? Does he have a tragic flaw in the spirit of Lear or Oedipus?

I have said as much, though it is a peculiar kind of flaw: the conviction that he spoke for God. It was the same flaw that brought down other American prophets like Anne Hutchinson, Nat Turner, and Martin Luther King. The flaw really, however, is within the American system. America cannot accept its own prophets. To rid the republic of its fanatical enemies (see question 9 below), its citizens have to resort to undemocratic means. That is what I meant by the phrase "the logic of the visionary life" in the introduction. We cannot reconcile our two founding documents: the Constitution and the Bible. One makes the people the voice of God, the other the prophets. The two are always in danger of clashing unless moderation is exercised on both sides.

9. RSR *gives considerable time to Joseph Smith's critics: Booth, Campbell, Howe, Bacheler, Turner, Bennett, and Law, among others. Was this choice conscious on your part? What do the critics have to teach us about Joseph Smith?*

Partly I was thinking of balance. The attacks on Joseph Smith were as much a part of his world as the testimonies of the believers. He lived under constant critical pressure; to understand his life, we must be aware of this harsh environment. Especially I wanted readers—Mormons and non-Mormons alike—to recognize the influence of the "fanatic" stereotype which I say at one point, with perhaps a little exaggeration, was as influential in American thought as racial stereotypes. People came with a preformed category of religious fanaticism that went back as far as Martin Luther and really beyond. It is part of the liberal mind to require adequate enemies who wish to crush all the liberal virtues of free speech and individual choice. The religious fanatic has served that purpose for hundreds of years and still does. This animus against fanaticism informs Jon Krakauer's book. Mormons are the enemy he loves to hate. Since the stereotype turns up in its full beauty in the writings of Joseph's critics, I wanted to give them voice.

10. *Joseph Smith's conception of a church of cities, rather than a church of congregations, you say at one point, was "doomed" in 1830s America (222). Despite the demise of Zion cities, the Zion idea has shown*

remarkable durability among believing Mormons for more than one hundred and fifty years. Why is Zion one of Joseph Smith's most resilient theological innovations?

A difficult question to answer. In New York City we are 20,000 people scattered in a population of 7 million. How can we consider ourselves in any sense a city? One reason may be the lasting force of the gathering. For sixty years we formed actual cities, and that may have engrained the communal concept into our cultural genes. (I think in general we have not adequately weighed the influence of that gathering period on our culture.) Another reason may be the continuing force of the word "consecration." The heart of Zion was the consecration of all our properties to God and each other. When we use that word in the temple, the memories of that complete consecration still play over the word. We are more committed to one another than other religious groups.

11. *Is Joseph Smith's kingdom-building useful in a post-9/11 world?*

What defines the post-9/11 world? Fear of terrorism, American militarism, Samuel Huntington-type cultural conflict? I think Joseph Smith's kingdom- building is useful in general. Perhaps its greatest use now is to restore calm and security, so that we do not take extreme measures. Knowing we have each other and the protection of God, we should continue to see all people as God's children and avoid rash action that will hurt more than it will help. Unfortunately, I am not sure it always works that way. Our apocalyptic tendencies take hold, and we look for the worst. We should be immune to panic but we are sometimes not.

12. *What does it mean to say that "the judgment of history has been that Joseph's great achievement was the creation of the Mormon people" (559)?*

By history I mean non-Mormon scholars who consider Joseph Smith's achievements after 200 years. They may dispute the scope and literary power of the Book of Mormon, dismiss Zion, the temples, priesthood, the doctrinal revolution and everything else, but they do not deny the people who came into being because of Joseph. At a discussion between evangelicals and Mormons at the American Academy of Religion in November 2004, Mark Noll said he considered Joseph Smith's claims to be "empty" but he could not gainsay the strength of the Mormon community.

13. *What are the practical consequences of the golden plates for appreciating Joseph Smith's place in American religious history? Are the plates an inevitable snag that get outside observers hung up on whether Joseph told the truth?*

The truth of the implied hypothesis is borne out by the Larry McMurtry review in the *New York Review of Books* (November 17, 2005). All McMurtry could talk about was the plates and plural marriage, the two most sensational points of Joseph's career. Nothing else about the Prophet interested him. I gave a talk at the Princeton Club about Joseph Smith in mid-October dealing with this very point. The problem with seeing Joseph Smith as a fraud, based on the gold plates story and plural marriage, is that it stops inquiry. He can be dismissed out of hand, and everything else he did is obscured.

November 14, 2005

Sitting at home at my computer in my little office in New York City. Flew in last night from Long Beach where I visited with Ben and gave talks at two versions of the Miller-Eccles study group. Sell-out crowds in both locations, the first at Morris and Dawn Thurston's huge mansion in La Villa Park, and the other at Russ Frandsen's, large but more modest house in La Cañada. About a hundred people at each occasion and all 150 copies of the book were sold. I sat and signed for a half hour or so at both houses. In other words a warm reception.

I left New York with four reviews in hand, by Julie Smith, Nate Oman, Russell Arben Fox, and Walter E. A. Van Beek of Leiden University, intended for publication on the Times and Seasons blog with replies from me. All were respectful and imaginative. It thrilled me to see other minds taking off from my work, to speculate about Joseph and his place in the world. It thrilled me that three were people I had not known before, offering hope that there are young LDS intellectuals in the making outside my ken. Then at the Thurstons, Armand Mauss handed me an outline of a talk given at the University of Utah LDS Institute by an anonymous reviewer. It expressed reservations, but was respectful throughout and basically accurate. Four major objections: (1) the book ascribes negative qualities to Joseph; (2) it gives too much weight to the influence of money-digging; (3) it describes Joseph Smith as developing into a prophet rather than being one from the start; (4) the language sometimes sounds as if Joseph invented his ideas rather than receiving them. I cannot object to any of those assertions. If that is the worst that conservatives do, I will feel fine. Giving too much weight to folk magic is a matter of judgment, but the others are factually true. The question is, Will they bother young Latter-day Saints? The reviewer says the book may cause problems as did Brodie's biography. He thinks conservatives will not like the book and moderates will struggle. I am curious to know if this prediction will prove to be true. In many cases, people say the book will bother someone else though they can take it themselves. I have gotten favorable comments from people all over the map religiously; are we merely imagining the young person troubled by hearing about all this stuff? The real question is, Should we hide troublesome things from the Saints and hope they will never find out? The problem then is what happens when they do. They are disillusioned and in danger of mistrusting everything they have been told. Frankly, I doubt if people will be horribly upset by anything critical here. The real problems are the violence in Missouri and polyandry. Amazingly, many LDS don't know Joseph married thirty women. We have to get these facts out to be dealt with; otherwise we are in a vulnerable position. It may be my job to bring the whole of Joseph's story into the open. The Institute people can work against the book if they choose, challenging the documents or offering explanations, but at least everything is on the table. We are not hiding anymore.

Claudia also relayed a comment of Mark Holden's following his recent visit to Kansas City. Mark, a New York City friend who collects Mormon documents and was talking to other collectors, found people who did not like the book. Either they thought it was too soft on Joseph or too hard. I suppose either criticism is correct. How am I to respond? My basic answer is that I tried to look at everything and then tell the truth as I saw it. Lots of people will disagree with where I came down, but I did the best I could as a historian and as a Latter-day Saint. Jed reports a big debate on one Mormon blog about my neglect of Helen Mar Kimball's marriage to Joseph. She was the famed fourteen-year-old that Krakauer makes so much of. But age is not the issue in Todd Compton's account of Joseph's plural wives. Compton highlights the stress the request for their daughter's hand put on the Kimballs, having to sacrifice their daughter to plural marriage, and on Helen herself, being deprived of her eligibility and social life at a young age. The interesting thing is that all this was told by Helen many years later when she had become a vocal defender of plural marriage. Why did I not include her story in the biography? The main reason is that I narrated Lucy Walker's wrestle with plural marriage which tells essentially the same story of a young girl fighting the

Prophet and then giving in. I also told Zina Huntington's story as an example of polyandry. I say that other accounts by plural wives follow the same pattern but don't mention Helen Mar Kimball. The reason for omitting her was not cover-up but a wish to avoid redundancy. How many such stories can you tell?

Where does all this leave me? A little buffeted to be sure, but not really disturbed. I knew in advance I would meet criticism. The enthusiasm greeting the book has exceeded my expectations. I hope I don't cause the General Authorities too much trouble. They doubtless are getting shocked reports from conservatives. I would not want this to lead to debates among themselves and needless fears. I am confident that in the long run the book will prove useful.

November 16, 2005

Perhaps it was Kim Smith, our Area Authority, who said yesterday I should write up my experiences in promoting this book to non-members. I silently agreed but realized I don't have much information on how the book is being read outside of Mormon circles. The small number of reviews have wandered all over the place, some fairly positive, but most emphasizing Joseph's exotic history more than I would like. A brief notice in the *New Yorker* today ended with a comment about a man with thirty wives. Mormons want Joseph to get the respect he never had before. I think that instead I am digging up the many layers of suspicion bordering on scorn. We get treated politely most of the time, so we live under the illusion Joseph is looked on respectfully. My serious effort to present him as a notable and honorable man brings out the hidden disrespect. I still am searching for the curious reader who is willing to be impressed by Joseph's achievements, but such a person may never show his face.

Jane Garrett at Knopf sent me a report from the Knopf team who tended the booth at the American Studies Association conference. They said mine was one of the strongest selling hard covers. At least that means someone besides Mormons is buying the book. But will they be persuaded? The *New Yorker* notice spoke of my treading the fine line between belief and objectivity, implying it is deucedly difficult if not impossible for a Mormon to write an "objective" book. I have recently been saying in my Mormon talks that the Book of Mormon is the strongest evidence both for Joseph Smith's inspiration and for his deceit. What defines a Mormon is our willingness to cross from disbelief to belief. In the world it is a very hard crossing, and the reactions to *RSR* show just how deep the gulf is. Mormons, including myself, think we are speaking rationally and persuasively about the Prophet when outsiders think we are in left field.

November 21, 2005

One of the happy by-products of the tours is meeting a new round of hosts. In Atlanta this past weekend, the governing spirit was a Latter-day Saint woman named Wendy Sharp, chair, I believe, of the local Public Affairs Committee. She attended to every detail and saw to it that nothing was lacking for our comfort, including a big fruit and candy basket when Claudia and I arrived at the Marriott Hotel. This was the last in the lecture series that began on September 30 in Springfield, Illinois, at the John Whitmer Historical Association meetings. I was gone every weekend through November 20, save for one in mid-October. Looking at the schedule in advance I wondered how I would get through it. Now looking back, it was not all that bad. I met a lot of people, signed hundreds of books, saw new country, gave many talks. My greatest concern throughout was selecting the right talk for the audience. Sometimes I was right on target; sometimes not. Talks that rang the bell in one location merely did the job elsewhere. In

Atlanta at Georgia State University, I spoke on "Joseph Smith and Creation of the Sacred," my Claremont talk. I was paired with Terryl Givens who repeated his Library of Congress address. I think we did the job pretty well there. On the other hand my "Life and Teachings of Joseph Smith" address that was such a success at Stanford, got a lukewarm response at the Powder Springs Stake center. I also spoke to a few dozen people at Gwinnett College, part of the state system, at 9:00 a.m. on Friday. I had not adequately prepared, thinking I could wing it and not knowing quite what to expect, and so fumbled around a little—a passable but not striking performance.

What am I learning from all these trips? Not a lot about the reception of the book. People buy it and ask to have it signed. The people who come up to me for a signature are complimentary. Tom Owens, the member of the stake presidency who put us up for the night in Powder Springs (with his wife, Heidi) asked questions about the seer stones and translation. Ordinary members are getting stuff they have not heard before and are a little uneasy at times. I am not surprised, considering that part of my purpose in writing is to introduce the troublesome material into the standard account to prevent horrible shocks later. On the other hand, I am also hearing the "nothing new" response. Glen Nelson mentioned this coming up in a BYU class, and Nate Oman gave his version in the Times and Seasons review. It follows from a question I have asked myself: What is new in the biography? People are looking for juicy little items they have never heard of before. Nate Oman said Fawn Brodie had all sorts of new revelations derived from Dale Morgan's research. After so much work on Joseph Smith, Oman thinks, we cannot expect any revelations of like magnitude. A similar attitude lay behind the comments of the four panelists at John Whitmer. They said that their view of Joseph Smith had not been changed by the book. Their response probably reflects a concentration on certain areas: an explanation of Joseph's revelations primarily.

Everyone is so hung up on the question of his prophetic authenticity that the new must bear on that issue or it does not count. Previously unexplored areas of his character, or a new conception of his prophetic role, or a new explication of his doctrine is not enough. As I wrote, I myself felt the lack of an overarching conception of his character and career, something equivalent to the notion of Irishness in a recent biography of the colonial administrator William Johnson. The author finds an Irish attitude informing his decisions and his perspective. What was the equivalent for Joseph Smith? I don't have a single theme to which I recur. I thought after the fact that I could have argued for the dominant influence of the Bible on a creative, independent mind. Joseph could be thought of as an imaginative person who had only the Bible among literary sources to feed his thinking. Unrestrained by an entrenched interpretive tradition or by institutional limits, his inspiration led him to passages and possibilities that more conventional minds could never have envisioned. That take on Joseph would have added a little coherence to the book and given reviewers something to chew on, but I doubt that it would have satisfied their search for something truly new. I feel strangely inhibited in locating some core interpretive structure. I can't seem to settle on anything. Is it my lack of imagination and analytical force, or am I being protected from making an error? Does a theme biography have a limited life, if only because no one angle on a person like Joseph is adequate to the man? I may be truer to his life by moving from one aspect to the next rather than by writing from a single commanding perspective. The biographies of Samuel Johnson and John D. Rockefeller, books I admire, don't emphasize one theme; they interweave many perspectives and are better for it.

Now a respite when I can get back to other projects. Meanwhile the reviews will trickle in, perhaps one in the *Times* eventually. The academic reviews will begin in a year or so. I am surprised there have not been more newspaper reviews, in California papers particularly where Mormons are a major presence. They may yet come to disturb my peace of mind.

November 30, 2005

For the past week I have suffered from bouts of depression interspersed with a strange lassitude. I have been unable to buckle down to my list of tasks. This and that has distracted me—checking the stock market, reading an article in the *New Yorker*, calculating my finances. For days very little has been accomplished though I sat at my desk the usual number of hours. Is this post-partum depression or travel fatigue? I felt no great relief in finishing up my round of travels. I don't think much about the book, though I do have a vague uneasiness about the negative responses that have surfaced. It is not as if I were fixated on the volume. Yet I have been unable to pull myself together. Even my mantra—"Today I will be a follow-er of Jesus Christ"—has had little effect. Nothing has been in focus.

Little by little I am establishing a new order to replace, first, the composition of the biography the dominant motif for eight years, and then preparation of talks, occupation for the past three months. I am working out how much time I should devote to reading the proposed annotation for History I in the Joseph Smith Papers, how much to work on my Annales farming paper, and so on. I hope to come back to life.

December 2, 2005

Occasionally I hear of critical comments emanating from the Church Educational System. The initials CES have come to represent a certain kind of highly conservative opinion in the

Church these days. For those who are slightly less staid, the term represents a kind of unbending stiffness that denies the realities. Actually there must be a variety of opinions among Institute teachers, many of whom are not strait-laced, but reservations about *RSR* may come to dominate the CES scene. Their negative views in turn will doubtless percolate up through the ranks of the General Authorities among those who share the CES preference for a slam dunk. Maybe I will hear repercussions, maybe not. In a way it does not matter. The book exists and will do its work whatever happens. People will mull over the facts about Joseph and eventually accommodate even the tough parts. In the end we will be more stable for having assimilated all this material. I may get beat up a little along the way; it goes with writing about Joseph Smith. But the book will do its work.

I continue to recover after the downer following the book tour. I am taking an interest in my work again and am more or less focused. The book is gradually receding from my consciousness, though the talks require me to keep Joseph Smith in mind.

December 3, 2005

Jane wrote to say the book has sold 43,664 copies thus far. At one time the figure would have astonished me. In the summer I feared the number would never reach 20,000, the point roughly where the advance is repaid. Now I don't know what to think. I suppose it is wonderful.

December 6, 2005

On the same day this week, I received letters from John Carmack and Marlin Jensen. Elder Carmack wrote to thank us for a $50 donation to the Perpetual Education Fund in the name of Gilbert Hutchings Sr., Gib's father, who just passed away. That was something in itself, but he went on to thank me for the Joseph Smith book. He was "deeply moved and touched" by the Kirtland Temple dedication chapter and apparently impressed with the Book of Abraham account, though I sensed he was still assimilating the idea of the translation being a revelation rather than an actual translation. At the end he spoke of my "brilliant and courageous book," causing me to wonder why he thought it courageous. Was I brave for trying to explain Joseph Smith to a doubting world or for taking on all the difficult passages in Joseph Smith's life on behalf of a Mormon audience? Probably the latter. Paul Peterson said the same about my chapter on plural marriage during a discussion at BYU a summer ago. I don't know if courageous is the word to describe my work in either case. I don't feel I am taking my life in my hands in either world. I certainly expect mixed reactions on both sides; but as I wrote, I was telling the story as I saw it. My concern was how to make Joseph intelligible to all kinds of readers, not to confront them in battle.

Marlin Jensen's letter told about meeting David McCullough. Elder Jensen and Rick Turley spoke to McCullough after a talk at Yale and promised to send him a copy of my book. In conveying the book they suggested McCullough take on westward migration as his next topic. With the letter to me, Elder Jensen included McCullough's handwritten note, saying thanks for the suggestion and mentioning that he was enjoying the book. Obviously McCullough is a very well brought up person.

Along the same lines, I spoke briefly with Elder Earl Tingey who was in New York to dedicate the Harlem chapel. He greeted me warmly and thanked me for my good work, not mentioning the book specifically. It is a sign of my sensitive temperament that I immediately interpreted his words as a reaction to the book. I figured he was saying indirectly, Your historical work is okay; you are not being frozen out. Perhaps in a few months I will stop reading every little gesture as a measure of approval and disapproval.

December 7, 2005

A note from Jane Garrett this morning. The book has gone into a third printing of 5,000 copies bringing the total to 56,000, a huge figure in my eyes, but not in the larger scheme of things. The *Times* this morning reported the disappointing sales of Martha Stewart's new book on how to run a business, just 37,000 copies. But then she had a two million dollar advance. One hundred thousand books was considered a high number in the calculations of the reporter. I won't reach that figure the first year but it may happen over the long haul as Jim Lucas once predicted. The Amazon ranking has been bouncing around between the 1200s and 600s, still a good number to my way of thinking. My advantage is that Mormons will buy the book for years to come, and it may eventually have some life in courses at BYU. Elise Soukup told me that the Joseph Smith *Newsweek* cover sold out in Utah despite having additional copies in stock. Mormons and non-Mormons alike in Utah buy up such things.

December 15, 2005

Yesterday I spoke on two talk shows, one hosted by Dennis Prager in Los Angeles, and the other a feature on NPR run by Howard Berkes, the network's western correspondent. (My taping of the Howard Berkes show to air on December 23 took place in NPR's New York studios at 801 Second Avenue. I spoke with Dennis Prager on the phone from our bedroom on the day when five windows in the apartment were being replaced. As I spoke great gaping holes opened to the twenty-degree air outside. Fortunately, it was cozy warm in our little bedroom.) I did not shine on either show though I more or less kept my head up. The day before, I was interviewed by Michael Kress of Beliefnet. We shall see how that turns out. I have not been in the best shape spiritually and that affects my composure and fluency. I was surprised on the Prager show to be accosted by evangelicals with their standard anti-Mormon questions. This morning I am thinking about how to answer. On the Berkes program, the big question was, How can a respectable scholar believe in Joseph Smith's extravagant claims? Berkes set me up for this query by having me relate just what Joseph Smith claimed to have happened to him in the early visions. I can't remember exactly what I said, but what I should have said is that many religions begin with a founding miracle—the parting of the Red Sea, the Resurrection—and these remain the most controversial and the most potent part of the faith. They seem impossible for outsiders to believe and at the same time are the strongest evidence of God's interest in humanity to believers. The gold plates are Mormonism's founding miracle. It is terribly hard to evaluate all these from a purely rational point of view, but you can look at the fruits of these claimed miracles. In my case, I like what Mormonism has produced. Mormon communities effectively help people to grow spiritually and serve one another. Because of their beliefs, Mormons give selflessly for a cause higher than themselves. Though far from perfect, Mormons do strive hard to be unselfish and to be better people. That seems to me to be confirmation of the value and religious truth of the founding experiences. I might add that what seems outlandish from the outside can appear quite rational from the inside. Mormon scholars have assembled lots of evidence for the authenticity of the Book of Mormon.

The one-shot question on the Prager show was, How many Gods are there? I answered, One, but could have added that Mormons believe in three Gods like other Christians, but we believe they are fully united in purpose and will, so that we speak of them as a single God. They are not contending personalities like the pantheon of Greek mythology. We also believe that humans can become like God, though what that means we cannot say. The scriptures do say that we are to seek to be perfect as our Father in Heaven is perfect and that we can be one with the Father as Christ is.

I can see that on my next guest appearance on the Neil Conan show, *Talk of the Nation*, I could be asked about God having a father. Yes, Joseph Smith did mention that in one sermon, but if we are to believe Christ's comment, there is still just one God in the sense of beings wholly united in mind and purpose.

What about God having been once a man? I can say that Christians certainly believe that. Christ is God and yet he was a man. That is a key feature of Christian belief, that God can come to earth in human form. Joseph Smith did say there were other worlds than this one, and that God came down to that earth as Christ came to this one.

Further possible question: Do Mormons believe we will have children in the hereafter? Yes, that is part of our affirmation of the body. God has a body; the body can be glorious, and so can having children. Parenting continues in the hereafter. Rearing children is what God is about, and so should we be.

Other questions. What are important religious teachings of Joseph Smith?

1. We can receive revelation.

2. All men can hold the priesthood and can act for God; women do, too, in certain circumstances.

3. We have divine potential.

In general, Mormon teachings reduce the separation between God and man. God is our instructor and Father, teaching us to become like him.

December 16, 2005

I woke up feeling bad this morning about my ungainly comments on the Howard Berkes show. I was not quite on target. Then the email contained a long letter from a Latter-day Saint in New Jersey objecting to my treatment of Joseph Sr. The man wrote with a friendly greeting and closing, but in between he was upset that I made Joseph's father look bad without sufficient justification. He also complained that I cited Fawn Brodie without referring to Hugh Nibley's rebuttal. Another email asked about my description of our doctrine of God on the Dennis Prager show in answer to a question. I can easily picture more email messages like this one. My New Jersey correspondent won't be happy when he gets to the pages on Joseph's character or his many wives. If I go off half-cocked in the interviews I am in for more complaints. I don't mind reactions to stuff I believe in, but the radio broadcasts are so susceptible to misstatements. I am formulating my reply as I give it and often get off the track a little. It is pretty lame to continually apologize for my own awkwardness. Sometimes I wish it would all go away, but it is likely to increase as readers get deeper into the book. They will begin to compare notes with others and build up criticism. They want to believe me because I am a brother; but if my opinions diverge too far from their own, they will rightfully complain.

It is a wearying prospect. It makes me realize that I am asking a lot from Church members. They want confirmation of their standard beliefs and I am forcing them to look at sides of Joseph's character they won't like. Forced to choose between me and their own ideas, I come out on the short end.

They are better off for knowing these things, but the transition to a fact-based understanding of the Prophet will be painful. I just have to keep calm. I can see that I may have already passed the high point of my popularity. From now on the negative stuff will come in. Besides the objections from Church members, there will be the academic reviews which are bound to include some heavy criticism. The doubters won't like my sympathetic approach. The book requires far more respect for Joseph Smith than they are willing to grant him. I will be stretched on the rack.

December 17, 2005

I awoke again with a heavy heart this morning with the memory of the Howard Berkes show still shadowing me. The consequence of these regrets, however, is a review of the questions and the formulation of better answers. As I sat in the temple last night after performing sealings for an hour or so, replies kept coming to mind. When I told Claudia about my struggles, she asked what my new answers were. I fumbled a little and came out with a few words, a reminder that a great answer in the head is not always a great answer in the mouth. You have to actually speak your brilliant thoughts before an audience. When you do, they may not work as well as you hoped. Here are a few of them.

1. Why do you believe the fantastic claims of an angel, plates, and translation?

Many religions are founded on miracles: the Jews and the deliverance from Egypt, the Christians with the Incarnation and Resurrection, Muslims and Mohammad's night journey to Jerusalem with Gabriel. The translation of the gold plates is Mormonism's founding miracle. Why some believe these miracles and others do not is a perplexing question. In my case, believing in them helps me to make sense of the world and to be a better person. It is like Jesus said in the New Testament: If you live his commandments, you will know if they be of God or if he spoke of himself. Living inside Mormonism, it all makes sense.

2. Why was Joseph Smith believable in 1830?

He took upon himself the role of prophet, which was entirely recognizable in his time. He lived in a society that valued the Bible above any other book, and the Bible is largely made up of the teachings of prophets. In Joseph Smith's time, people were hoping and praying for a return of prophetic revelation. They wanted to enjoy the gifts of the Bible. When he said God had spoken to him, they were ready to believe.

3. What is Joseph Smith's meaning to the Church today?

Joseph Smith is a combination of Martin Luther and Saint Peter. He offered a new way of believing and living Christianity as Luther did for the Protestants; and he was the basis of authority for all the succeeding leaders of the Church as Saint Peter is for the Popes. They all derive their authority from the original commission of Christ to Peter: Upon this rock, I will build my church. Smith received a similar commission from heavenly visitors.

4. What are Joseph Smith's distinctive religious teachings?

We must remember that he did not set out to form a new religion. He taught the Christian message but with new emphases rather than creating something entirely new. One of these emphases was the importance of ongoing revelation, beginning with himself, continuing to all the presidents of the church who succeeded him, and extending to every member. Everyone was to seek revelation for themselves, their families, and their callings in life. Joseph Smith's own revelation opened the possibility of closer communication with heaven.

He also taught, following the Bible, that man is created in God's image, interpreting that to mean God has a human form. He is not some abstract spiritual force but an actual person.

A third teaching was a restoration of priesthood, authority and power from God to act in his name. This priesthood was not reserved for a special class of priests but extended to all worthy men.

These three have the effect of bringing people closer to God, making him more accessible, encouraging people to seek him out, try to be like him, and to act for God in all their relationships with one another.

5. How many Gods do you believe in?

Like all Christians, the answer is one and three. There are three persons in the godhead—Father, Son, and Holy Ghost. Yet they are all one—in mind and purpose, we believe, though not in substance. We also believe man can become like God, therefore adding to the number of gods, but once again they are unified, as Christ in John 17:21 said they would be—as he and his Father were one.

When I awoke, I was also feeling bad because of losing focus. I have not been praying with concentration and in talking with people have been flip and light-minded. Yet out of these discontents come new thoughts, new ways of speaking—not that light-mindedness fosters creative thinking, but I feel the need to seek. The uneasiness has kept me striving. When I wake with pain in my heart, my mind starts reviewing the problems and seeking a closer focus on Christ. It was probably not coincidental that some of the best thoughts came in the temple last night.

One further thought: I watched President Bush's interview with Jim Lehrer before going to the temple last night. He seemed unsure and forced in his answers. Trying to figure out why, I thought it is partly because he usually speaks to friendly audiences. Sitting before a reporter who was going to be more critical, he faltered, and I do the same. I also thought it was partly because he is not entirely honest. He keeps thinking of the criticisms of his statements and is not certain he is answering satisfactorily. As I watched I was of course applying these observations to myself. I need to be perfectly honest when I speak, saying only what I believe and can truthfully speak before any audience, no matter how critical.

December 20, 2005

I visited the NPR New York studios again yesterday. They are at 801 2nd Avenue between 42nd and 43rd. This time I had approximately an hour with Neil Conan on *Talk of the Nation*. It actually was more like forty minutes. The show began with five minutes of news and ended with a ten-minute piece on the Ibox, a new toy of some kind. Along the way there were musical interludes. I was alone with Conan for ten minutes or so and then he turned to questions. After about twenty minutes, Mario De Pillis came on from an Amherst studio. One questioner wanted to know about Fawn Brodie's *No Man Knows My History*. A Salt Lake caller complained about our celebrating Joseph Smith's birthday instead of Christ's and said many young Latter-day Saint were giving up on the fabulous story of the plates. The final caller asked about Joseph's 33 wives and 11 polyandrous relationships. Conan wanted to know about the conditions that produced Joseph Smith. I felt he was basically sympathetic. At one point he helped me answer the question about believing the plates story by referring to a key passage in my book where I talk about following the story of believers rather than the story of skeptics.

I felt that I came through pretty much unscathed. Claudia said I sounded strong. She likes it when I don't stutter but come out with complete sentences. She thought Mario talked too slowly and didn't have a lot to say; he sounded wise to me. Doug Bunker from Buffalo called to say he liked the show, and I got an email from someone in Seattle who heard it and liked it. I wrote back that you don't have much of a chance to promote the Church in these situations; you just try to keep your head up. I did walk away happily from the interview and woke up feeling happy. It was an antidote to the Howard Berkes interview.

The best thing was that I had concentrated on remaining composed that day and fairly well succeeded. During the show I kept repeating my mantra and figure it helped. This morning the URL for the show was published on the online news service LDS Today along with a favorable review of the book in the *Christian Science Monitor*. Overall I think it was the best review I have received. Not that it was filled with praise, but it seemed to understand what I was up to. Claudia had also sent in a report on the Joseph Smith statue dedication to LDS Today, and they made it the lead story. Overall a good day.

December 22, 2005

I went to sleep feeling at ease and woke up in the same spirit, having slept a full eight hours. My interview for KUER, the NPR station at the University of Utah in Salt Lake went smoothly. No hostile questions and pretty good answers. The host was basically sympathetic, I thought. One of the questions was, Why tell readers I am Mormon? Wouldn't the book have been more credible without the confession? He may be right. Reviewers always mention that I am a believer. Maybe I should have left them guessing the way Terryl does. The questioner pointed out that Fawn Brodie does not admit that she was a lapsed Mormon fighting her way clear of the Church. Is not that as relevant as my believing status? All I said is that I am confessional by nature, and that I did not make a big point of my faith in the book, mentioning it only in one sentence. I suppose that I want people to know I am a believer. Mormons certainly are more willing to accept a work from a member, and it has always been my way to clarify my position.

I spoke from the Carnegie Recording Studios right in Carnegie Hall. The man in charge records Carnegie concerts and travels around the world doing live concerts using his own equipment. Feeling good I walked home from 56th Street to our place at 118th, coming through Central Park from 59th to 110th. It was a bright, crisp day and I passed through sections of the park I had never seen. When I got here an email from Jane Garrett reported that the book has gone into a fourth printing. Another 10,000 copies brings the total to 66,000. My only response to her was, "Wow!" I never imagined that many books would sell. Curt Bench thought 20,000 would be a large number. Knopf must be surprised too, considering that they keep going back rather than printing more initially. Some day I would like to know where the books are actually being produced.

December 25, 2005

Another mellow day. It feels a little like the end of an era as well as the end of a year. I have wrapped up the interviews and major talks. The book is now doing its own work. Today I remembered the Evans Biography Award for books in Mormon and Western history. I wrote Jane to ask if Knopf was aware of the prize and had submitted a copy. She had no idea. Unfortunately, the books were due on

December 1. On the other hand, it would be no loss if *RSR* was not considered. I received an Evans prize for *Joseph Smith and the Beginnings of Mormonism*. It might be awkward to give the prize again for an extension of the same book. Greg Prince's McKay biography would be a worthy recipient in any event.

I doubt if there will be many more newspaper reviews. It looks as if the *New York Times* is going to stiff the book. The reviews in Mormon journals will come along next and then the academic reviews. My inclination is to keep still. A seminary teacher in California wrote to complain about a review by Jane Lampman in the *Christian Science Monitor* that was republished in his local paper. He had found twelve errors in her account and wanted me to challenge her. I told him the review was more moderate than many I had read. People pretty much find the Joseph Smith they want in the book. Much of what he objected to was the spin, not the facts. I urged him to read the book and tell me what he thought.

What I would like most is to let Joseph Smith subside for a time. I want to clear my head entirely and turn to other labors. After a fallow period, I can take up the topic again. Right now I feel as if I am in a rut. I want a fresh start.

December 30, 2005

I received a letter asking about Joseph Smith's marriages to married women, one of the most perplexing parts of his life. This one is hard to understand, and I said as much in my reply.

> I fear I have little to offer by way of explaining polyandry. It remains a puzzle. All I know is that Joseph Smith was preoccupied with sealing—not just husbands to wives, but

children to parents, and one generation to another. He wanted to lock people into relationships—not necessarily sentimental relationships but ones of mutual obligation and cooperation. Our preoccupation with romance blocks us, I think, from understanding what he was getting at. I am sure he had affection for his wives, but marriage as a culmination of a powerful attraction was not his point. He saw marriage as the formation of a relationship that would in some way make people responsible to one another. All of this was connected in turn with raising up a people. Another element is his concern for lineage—that priesthood comes down by lineage. Forming the right kinds of line or being linked to the right lines facilitates that transmission.

None of this is satisfactory for us, but I hope that you don't make it a matter of belief or unbelief, but of inquiry. There is something more here to be discovered. Was Joseph pointing toward something we would benefit from knowing? In that latter part of your letter, you seem to be moving in that direction-speculating on the possibilities. I hope you write these things down. One good way to begin is to write out the problem in its most acute form. What precisely bothers you about Fannie Alger and the later polyandry? What is so wrong about these relationships? Then work your way back from there. Speculate on how Joseph might have answered your criticisms. What did they look like from his point of view?

All the best,

Richard Bushman

Notes

1 The paper, "Joseph Smith's Many Histories," was later published in the proceedings of the conference, *The Worlds of Joseph Smith*, in *BYU Studies* 44, no. 4 (2005): 3–20.

2 "Joseph Smith and Abraham Lincoln," *Joseph Smith and the Doctrinal Restoration: The 34th Annual Sidney B. Sperry Symposium* (Provo, Utah: Brigham Young University, Religious Studies Center/Salt Lake City: Deseret Book, 2005): 89–108.

End of the Run: January–May 2006

January 8, 2006

I received a personal note about *RSR* from a retired General Authority yesterday. It came in a small envelope from his home address and was signed with his first name—definitely not an official communication. He called the book a "monumental accumulation of references from a multitude of sources." In the second paragraph, he expressed his "disappointment in the balance presented between the negative and the positive." He thought opponents of the Restoration will find additional fuel and that newly converted or marginal Saints may be weakened. He also objected to the debunking of significant figures in the Restoration. Obviously he had been thinking about the book and had many worries. I wrote to say my only aim was to tell a truthful story based on all the sources. The problem with the fuel-for-enemies objection is that the fuel is already there. I don't provide it. We have to deal with it or it will be used against us.

My correspondent must speak for many General Authorities and CES teachers. My Joseph is so far removed from theirs they cannot help but object. If he speaks for other influential Church leaders, I may be in for rough times. I marvel that I have survived to this point, considering that my first book brought up many of the same problems. Whether or not I go down, I think the Church will find the book useful when they need a more objective account. I am quite willing to let the book do its work without official approval. The overall effect will be to move the Church toward greater candor, even though I suffer in the mean time. I am concerned about the discrepancy between the idealized Joseph in Institute classes and the criticized Joseph in secular and hostile sources. Young Latter-day Saints are left to reconcile these two without help from their teachers. Simply denying the validity of the criticism is not enough when facts are involved. Some will shut their minds to the criticism; but others will become disillusioned, not just with the Prophet but with the entire teaching apparatus. They will feel they have been misled. My book may encourage a dialogue about candor within CES. The instructors will ask each other what is lost and gained by telling the full story. Gradually the center of opinion will move toward openness.

[On the topic of General Authority reactions, I wrote this letter to Elder Holland after receiving the January/February 2006 issue of *Books and Culture* with a review by Laurie Maffly-Kipp.]

Dear Elder Holland:

The first of the serious reviews of *Joseph Smith: Rough Stone Rolling* arrived this past week. You may see *Books and Culture*, the evangelical equivalent of the *New York Review of Books*, but I send it along in case this issue has not caught up with you. Laurie F. Maffly-Kipp's reaction to my book is probably about as sympathetic as we can hope for. You probably know that she offers a seminar on Mormonism at the University of North Carolina and attracts Mormon graduate students because of her empathetic approach. She is now writing a general survey of Mormonism.

The review tells me that we cannot expect a positive reaction to the biography—or to Joseph Smith—from scholars. As Laurie says, an epistemological gap yawns between my view of the Prophet and that of most academics. Believing Mormons stand on the other side of a gulf separating us from most educated people. I was surprised that she would not allow for the possibility of a visionary American in the tradition of the world's great visionaries.   Instead she requires a naturalistic explanation.

I was more surprised that she considered my presentation of his character too "rosy." If anything, Mormon reaction is the opposite. While most Latter-day Saint readers enjoy an unvarnished account of his life, others are unsettled by the rough spots.   One correspondent, probably speaking for many CES people, wrote saying he thinks I am too hard on Joseph and other early Saints. Laurie sees none of this.

Even this self-proclaimed sympathetic observer thinks I gloss over his flaws. It suggests that many informed academics think of Joseph as a shady character. I see the hand of Brodie in this response. Brodie has shaped the view of the Prophet for half a century. Nothing we have written has challenged her domination. I had hoped my book would displace hers, but at best it will only be a contender in the ring, whereas before she reigned unchallenged.

Frankly, I had hoped for better from Laurie and from the academy in general. But these are the facts of life. While we get smiles and toleration in many of our relationships, below the surface is deep disagreement, even a touch of hostility. We suffer from this disparity. I keep hearing of young people who are shocked to discover the ideal Joseph Smith they learned about in Church is not the Joseph Smith most scholars perceive. Taken aback, the young Mormons not only wonder about the Prophet but about their teachers. Everything comes tumbling down. I had hoped my book would bridge this gap, but after this review, I can see it will go only part way. I will be consistently seen as a partisan observer.

Thanks for the listening ear.   I also enclose Gerald McDermott's analysis of Mormonism as a world religion.

McDermott is a conservative scholar who has written on Jonathan Edwards and world religions. He deflates some of Rodney Stark's more extravagant claims.

Thank you for your friendship.

Warm regards,

Richard

January 17, 2006

I flew back from Seattle yesterday. I had gone out on the invitation of Molly Bennion to speak in the Seattle Stake. I spent a night with Ann and John Romish, who recently moved from Portland to Seattle to be nearer their son, John Andrew. Owen and Barbara Clark came to a dinner at the Bennions just before the talk. It was another case of meeting old friends through the book.

The Seattle trip coincided with the long-delayed *New York Times* review. Jane Garrett had sent me an advance copy earlier in the week, so there were no surprises on Sunday. My reaction to the review itself was somewhat prejudiced by the history of the reviewer. Walter Kirn had joined the Church in his teens and then faded in his young adulthood. I first encountered him through a *New Yorker* short story about a Mormon youth trip. I thought the story was vicious. He wrote another long piece about his experience with Mormonism, explaining his conversion and later defection. I thought this was another case like Brodie's where personal history sours the author's outlook on the Prophet. Claudia, however, reacted differently. She thought Kirn took Joseph seriously, possibly because Kirn was once a Mormon. Jed Woodworth was even more enthusiastic.

The *NY Times* came through! Did you see the *Times* review by Walter Kirn? (http://www.nytimes.com/2006/

01/15/books/review/15kirn.html) I am thrilled with this review, by my sights the best published yet. What I like so much is the pragmatic complexity in the writing. Nothing is simple—not Smith's visions, not his movements, not Bushman's goals. Unlike Larry McMurtry, who works hard to entertain, Kirn dives into the extremities and contradictions of Smith's life. He ventures pragmatic explanations, not final judgments. . . .

The last paragraph with its reference to Santa Claus went south for me, but I do think it exposes the perils of rationalizing Mormonism's importance through reference to growth statistics. We have to keep looking for ways to justify our significance without reference to our own success, which has always incited fear, then as now.

Those two reactions have mollified me a little. At least I have not been publicly shamed as I feared I would be in the *Times*. I did notice last night that the Amazon orders went up on the Monday following the Sunday review. I hope that means a few non-Mormons are trying the book.

January 28, 2006

One lovely letter yesterday from Kent Nielsen, my Harvard roommate, and a historian of science. He said he rejoiced on reading "Stories of Eternity." His reaction doubly pleased me, because that is the chapter where I speculate about Copernican and Ptolemaic astronomy, something he knows a lot about. He also is a lover of the mysteries explicated in that chapter. Others have commented favorably on the doctrinal chapters. They may be the Mormon favorites.

February 6, 2006

Elder Holland wrote a generous note last week. I was pleased to have him say "You knew (and I knew and everybody else knew) that you would have to deal with things as honestly and forthrightly as you could. Nevertheless, your faith and loyalty are apparent on every page." That implies General Authorities appreciate the value of candor. I no longer worry about an effort to close down the book. There remains the problem of becoming a rival expert in the interpretation of doctrine, but I can avoid that by not talking doctrine when asked to speak. My mind is aswirl with doctrinal ideas which do not need to be vented, especially when I acknowledge their speculative nature myself.

The book seems to be cutting its own path now, just as hoped. I hear of people moved by it; others read it twice to get it straight. This tells me that people are adjusting their own images of the Prophet to take all the new material into account. I sense they are challenged but not struck down by what they learn.

Actually the whole episode is fading, like the dead gradually forgetting the living in *Our Town*. I am moving into other spheres. Unfortunately, this book like every other book will pursue me for years. I have to talk about it at the Mormon History Association and there are all these talks coming up over the next few months. The Chemical Engineering Department at BYU has signed me up to talk to their alumni next fall. I don't really mind. I have two or three pretty good talks to choose from and in a few hours can get one of them revved up. I meet new people at each event. Gradually I will develop new talks, probably based on the reviews. Appointments to talk to the University of Utah Institute and to the Joseph Smith Papers staff while in Utah later in the month have generated a few new thoughts.

I wrote to Elder Holland about a rough patch ahead as animosity to religion keeps growing. I am coming to envision a new persona for the Church as humble followers of Jesus Christ. Instead of speaking triumphantly of the gospel sweeping the earth, could we think of ourselves as the leaven in the lump, standing for righteousness and serving others? I wish we had a long record of kindness and friendship to fall back on, with less stress on proselyting. Then when the storms break around us, we would have friends to turn to. Our covenant with God is to bless the people of the earth. That should be our motto. Establishing Zion does not mean sweeping vast masses of people onto our membership records but creating a people of God dedicated to blessing others. Joseph and his early followers came forth with lots of triumphalist rhetoric, but I think we need a new voice, one of humility, friendship, and service. We should teach people to believe in God because it will soften their hearts and make them more willing to serve.

February 15, 2006

Last week I learned that *RSR* will be awarded the Association for Mormon Letters biography award next week. Since I will be in Utah, I can attend its meetings at Utah Valley State College to receive the award in person. It is probably relevant that I failed to mention the notification in this journal. I am withdrawing from the book. Its fate no longer means as much as it first did. I am insulated from every kind of shock by the book's sales success and the warm reception from Mormons. People keep writing and commenting, almost all positively. With that behind me, the negatives don't register very high on the Richter scale and neither do the positives. I know where the book sits in the larger scheme of themes. I am happy with the reception but not elated—just calm about it. I am ready to move on to other things.

February 28, 2006

Back in New York after a week in Utah and Idaho. Pretty much wall-to-wall talks: Cottonwood Stake on Tuesday,

BYU-Idaho on Thursday, University of Utah Institute and students on Friday, Utah State Prison and Ensign Stake on Sunday. On Saturday, I received the Association for Mormon Letters biography award at the meeting at Utah Valley State College. On Wednesday I admitted participants to the BYU summer seminar on Mormon Thought that Terryl Givens and I will run. Lots of people reading the book. Many came up for signatures.

I am coming to the conclusion that this is a phenomenon, not just a successful book. I seem to have struck a chord. People were ready for this kind of Joseph Smith. I speculated at various times during the week about a transition in Mormon culture. We have caught up with a general departure from the heroic and idealistic. We want the gritty and real as does the rest of the world. Spotless characters don't appeal. I also sense a hunger for down-to-earth talk. Since people live in the real world, they know the idealistic talk of our sermons is another order of speech. Like the talk of partisan politicians, it has to be discounted. Readers are relieved to hear Joseph Smith discussed in ordinary language. Even the University of Utah Institute teachers went along with my view on the necessity of telling students the whole story. I was expecting a negative reaction and counted on Mormon "nice" to preserve me from their attacks. No attacks were made; and what is more, many affirmations of the importance of realism were voiced. John Peterson, the person who invited me, told me afterward the faculty were pleased with the presentation, especially because at the end I raised my old problem of teaching kids about the atonement to deal with their sins. I suppose they got a sense of my concern for the souls of young people.

Problems during the week: I have a tendency to moan about the inability of scholars to go along with my suspension of disbelief and complain about the failure of secular minds to appreciate Joseph Smith. I think I am secretly asking for pity. You don't understand how hard it is for me, I seem to be saying. Such whimpering is never good. The worst mistake was Sunday's Ensign Stake talk. At the end I did not bear my testimony. On other occasions, I have had audience members ask me about my testimony. LDS audiences always want to know. Someone came up to me afterward and asked if I ever bore my testimony to these groups. On another occasion a person asked me if I was a patriarch. He wanted to assure a reader of my book that I must have a testimony if I was. On Sunday a man who hung around for a long time finally said, I bet your testimony is different from that of people in this room. I said it was, but that I believed in the gold plates. He was astounded. I must find a way of conveying my basic belief in all these settings. I felt bad after the Ensign Stake talk and am still mourning a little. Partly this is vanity; people were not as enthusiastic as in Cottonwood. But partly it is a realization that I have erred and must improve my ways.

As for the Association for Mormon Letters award, I feel pretty neutral about such things. The reception of the book by Mormon readers makes me immune from other kinds of rewards and punishments. Lark Evans Galli, a member of the Evans Prize committee, wrote to ask me to resign from their board so that my book could be considered for the prize. I happily agreed, not feeling one way or another about the prize. All in all, I seem to be most concerned about talking effectively about Joseph. The book can take care of itself.

March 4, 2006

I don't know quite what to say about my trip to North Carolina these past two days. A graduate student in religion, Ariel Bybee Laughton, niece of our Ariel Bybee, the Metropolitan Opera singer, arranged for a talk at Duke followed by a fireside the next day at the University of North Carolina Institute. I gave my "Many Lives of Joseph Smith" talk at Duke and "Translation of the Book of Mormon" at the Institute. Both are tried and true talks, given perhaps a half dozen times before. But somehow they both were a little flat. I don't know exactly why. Was I not humble and spiritual enough? Did they lack testimony-bearing in the appropriate spots? Were they too shocking to the audiences? At Duke, 95 percent of the listeners were LDS as usual. Perhaps "Many Lives" does not work well for Church members. I sensed the same flatness at the Ensign Stake last Sunday with the same talk. In fact beginning that day, none of my talks have been as punchy as I would like. Today I am fasting for light on this matter. One side of me says to just soldier on, think spiritually, do your best, let the chips fall. The other says, Take action. Strengthen your spirit, reconceive the talks, bear testimony more. Once again at the Institute, one of the questioners asked me at the end to explain my testimony. As it so happens, the bishop in the Inwood 3 singles ward has asked me to talk on my testimony of Joseph Smith next Sunday during my scheduled visit as a high council speaker. Perhaps that will clarify my thinking. Right now I seem to be working on all fronts— rethinking the talks, examining my soul, praying for help. I keep thinking of the story of President McKay complaining to his secretary Clare Middlemiss that he could not understand why he didn't have the Spirit during a conference talk when he had made every effort to be humble.

Ariel spoke of various LDS graduate students in religion who were drifting away from the Church. The bishop's request for a talk on Joseph Smith in Inwood suggests that the same thing may be happening in his ward. I proposed to Ariel that we should have a conference of divinity school students at Duke/UNC, Yale, and Harvard to discuss their common problems. Perhaps we need a time for more talk of this kind in our stake.

March 16, 2006

I sometimes get letters from people who are wavering. They still believe in the Prophet but have troubling questions. One wrote: "I have become somewhat troubled at the feelings I have developed as I have studied Joseph Smith. I find myself understanding, but not sympathizing with, those who opposed him. At times I wonder how I would have reacted to his doctrinal developments in Nauvoo. What would I have done if he had proposed to my wife?"

My reply:

> I can imagine how questions about Joseph Smith's life could trouble you. You want to be loyal to what you have known, and yet certain episodes and aspects are disturbing. I personally think it is never good to let problems like this swim vaguely around in your head. I would take the top three and write them down. And I don't mean just in a list, but describe exactly what happened and why this bothers you. Be sure you get all the facts right, not just from negative books but from more sympathetic accounts like my biography. Consider the biases, both pro and con, of those who describe the events. Then ask yourself, Why does this seem contrary to what a prophet would do? What exactly is wrong with this?

> At the same time, to be fair, you should ask yourself, Did Joseph do anything that shows him to be worthy to be called a prophet? Is there anything that seems admirable, heroic, or miraculous? Apart from your feelings about him, what are his actual accomplishments? Are these in keeping with his prophetic role? Try to be hard-headed about this. Don't let your feelings swamp you.

> While you do this, you must be living right. You can't be breaking the commandments yourself and expect to get a clear view of Joseph's life (John 7:16-17). Guilt clouds the

mind. If you are knowingly sinning, you will subconsciously want to separate yourself from God and find reasons for denying his power.

If you are going to do all this in the Latter-day Saint way, you will also put your trust in that Spirit that leadeth to do good (D&C 11:12-14). You will ask, What are the consequences of these beliefs? Have they resulted in good in your own life and the life of others you have known? If they have, then you want to treat them with respect. As with science, a religion that works and produces results has to be taken seriously.

Others might give you other advice, but this has worked for me. After all these years of studying Joseph's life, I believe more than ever.

All the best,

Richard Bushman

March 29, 2006

A few days ago I received official notice of the Evans Biography Award from the Mountain West Center. The news had been relayed even before then by email, and I expressed my thanks. That day when Claudia came home, I forgot to tell her until she read my email. Not until today have I brought myself to make an entry in this journal. Why the lassitude? I am not sure the prize should rightfully go to me. I was awarded half of the Evans prize in 1985 for publishing *Joseph Smith and the Beginnings of Mormonism*; the other half went to Linda Newell and Val Avery for their biography of Emma Smith, *Mormon Enigma*. Four chapters from *Beginnings* carried over to *RSR*. Besides the duplication, Greg Prince's biography of David O. McKay is a worthy recipient. The Mountain West Center letter did report he was receiving the Evans Handcart Award.

Beyond questions about the justice of the award, lassitude has set in from other quarters. Today during a conference call with the Smith Papers staff, Grant Underwood was making a point about the impossibility of pleasing everyone and cited my book as an example. You work hard and get mixed reviews. That seems to be the final outcome. Lots of Mormons like the book. Non-Mormon readers are lukewarm or skeptical. We have to content ourselves with polite respect and little more. No one outside of the Mormons is taking Joseph Smith seriously. I cite Bloom over and over, but he is a lone voice that goes unheard. At the Library of Congress symposium, scholars took Joseph seriously for purposes of discussion, but they don't see in him prophetic qualities or even flashes of genius. He is a phenomenon only. I will try again at Columbia's Lehman Center next month, though I doubt that many Americanists will come to listen. Who wants to know more about Joseph Smith? In most minds, he is an outlier or a horrible example and little more.

After the BYU symposium, I decided I must brighten up my aspect. No longer droop in despair. The fact is that we are being talked about. The book was reviewed both in the *Times* and the *New York Review of Books*. Joseph demands at least that much attention. It is significant that we are talking to scholars. They can't dismiss the entire Mormon scholarly establishment. Little by little they may understand there was more to Joseph Smith than extravagant claims about angels and gold plates. We have to do our job better, too, which we will learn if we keep trying.

I spoke in Dallas to the Texas edition of the Miller-Eccles fireside and to the Plano Stake last weekend. For the stake audience, I wrote a new talk, "Joseph Smith's Relationship to God." It came out of a request from a stake president in Salt Lake City who is sponsoring a talk on April 9 to say something about JS holding on when things were going bad. That thought combined with elements of other addresses added up to something that fits the title. I outlined the talk on the plane, filled in the outline on the Davidsons' computer, and photocopied pages from their copy of *RSR* to supply the quotations. It got a pretty good response from the crowd, enough new perspectives to satisfy their curiosity and enough spiritual direction to give the talk a sermonic feel. I will work it over again before April 9. The two sessions in Plano restored my confidence which had slipped after my recent talks, none of which was quite on target. I felt the lack of a spiritual note in my talks on translation. This talk rights the balance. Steve and Daryl Eccles were my hosts in Plano; C. Bruce Jones is the stake president.

April 12, 2006

During my trip to Utah, I heard from Richard Sadler that my book has been awarded the Best Book prize by the Mormon History Association. I was at Weber State to give a lecture at an event sponsored by the College of Social Sciences and two local historical societies. It was a huge evening—probably 350 people there, jamming the aisles, sitting on the dais, and overflowing into the halls. Afterwards I signed books for half an hour. A few people came from Salt Lake City to hear the talk. The response so overwhelmed me that I forgot to tell Claudia about the prize, another example of my distance from the book. At this point, I am more involved in the ongoing lectures than the fate of the book. I also have to think about the sessions where my work is to be discussed at historical conferences. At the Mormon History Association meetings in May, a panel consisting of Dan Vogel, Bill Russell, Gary Topping, and Martha Bradley is going to comment. I am trying to decide how to respond to the criticism this gang of four is likely to come up with. Martha will be the only sympathetic panelist, and she will get on me for not saying more about women. I don't know what the others will say. I have also been approached by John Van Engen, a medievalist whom I met at Princeton's Davis Center years ago, to hold a session on my book at the American Society of Church History meetings next January, to which I have agreed. Once more a roasting. That will make four in all I will have undergone.

April 18, 2006

At Kenneth Jackson's invitation, I talked about Joseph Smith at the newly revived Lehman Center at Columbia today. About fifteen people turned up for lunch and discussion, including Casey Blake, Andy Delbanco, Herbert Sloan, and a flock of graduate students. I talked about the problems of accessing Joseph Smith because of the characterization of him as a charlatan. Hard to take him seriously and so Joseph Smith is never examined closely. I further mused why the Book of Mormon does not have a place in American cultural history courses and discussed the problem it presents: Why an apocryphal Bible in the nineteenth century from a rural Yankee? The questioning was pretty good. Lots of interest in the subject, but even more in me. Andy wanted to know my relationship to the Book of Mormon. Someone else asked how my close study of Joseph Smith affected my personal view of him. Ken Jackson talked about his own experience after his son died and how he realized he needed something more to understand life than what Columbia offered. There were many opportunities—actually eager invitations—for me to talk about my own religious belief and my convictions about the Book of Mormon. I did say that I had discovered over many years that I am a believer. I want to believe in God and I do believe in God. I said moreover that I did not think Joseph Smith was capable of writing the Book of Mormon— the book was too complex—and that how it came about remains a mystery. These were not bad answers under the circumstances, but I felt I could have been more forthright.

What would I say if given the chance again? To my other replies, I think I would add that religious texts have always served to orient and comfort people. They have a way of inducing contemplation and a striving for a better life. The Book of Mormon serves that purpose for me. It does yield to devotional reading. This is true for most Mormons and certainly for me. In other words, it functions as the Word of God the way the Qur'an and the Bible do. I believe it is true in the deepest sense. Its remarkable origins do not faze me. I am quite open to the possibility that it all happened exactly the way Joseph Smith said it did. I think Joseph Smith was a truth-teller. Angels do not seem like an impossibility to me—nor gold plates. But what attracts me most strongly is the inspiration I find in the text itself.

April 19, 2006

In a letter to the *New York Review of Books* that I can't find, Larry McMurtry replies to the critics of his earlier review of my book. He compares my biography to Fawn Brodie's much to her advantage. She is far the better writer, McMurtry says. My book lacks "kick"; and if there is one thing a biography of Joseph Smith must have, it is "kick." Moreover, he goes on, Brodie recognizes that Mormonism is based on a fraud while Bushman "plays pitty-pat" with the question of authenticity.

I thought of those words this morning as I went on reflecting about my answer to the question of my relationship to the Book of Mormon. Am I afraid to come down unequivocally for fear of cutting myself completely out of the academic discussion, like a Jew covering up his Jewishness or a pale African American trying to pass? I say to myself that I confess my belief on the opening page, and from there on I am simply trying to make room for a non-believer. Long ago I said on a radio interview that Fawn Brodie cuts Mormons out

of her book. There was no room for believers among her readers unless they accepted the status of idiots and dupes. I did-
n't want to leave non-Mormons out of my account, so I tried
to address them and say, I understand your needs. Do I go so
far in this direction in *RSR* that I play pitty-pat? In my effort
to make the Book of Mormon intelligible, do I fail to convey
my own conviction that it is true? And the same for the revelations and for Joseph Smith's divine calling.

Somehow I felt like I was playing pitty-pat yesterday at the
Lehman Center. I fell somewhere short of complete unequiv-
ocality in my answers. I have thought of many better answers
since. Perhaps the best is the simplest: "Yes, I believe the
Book of Mormon is true. I am a Mormon; that is what
Mormons do." Or on another tack: "Yes, I believe Joseph
Smith's story. I don't think he was a fraud." Or: "Yes, I believe
the Book of Mormon is true. That is why I want it to be
treated with more respect. Whether you believe it or not, the
book is a marvelous creation." These answers retreat into the
personal like most testimonies. They don't assert that everyone must accept my truth; they call it my truth, implying you
can have your truth. I am simply presenting my point of view;
take it or leave it. The advantage of listening to my point of
view is that you can come to understand what it was like to be
a Mormon or to be Joseph Smith.

I can see now that I could have written the whole book inside
this framework. Instead of trying to keep the reader and
myself in the same place, creating a common point of view
amenable to believer and non-believer alike, I could have taken
on the role of guide to a Mormon perspective on the Mormon
prophet, acknowledging the differences and saying, This is
how we look at it. The point of persuasion would be to show
the benefits of examining Joseph from a believer's perspective.
What can you learn by looking at him through believing eyes
that might be lost if you begin with the assumption he had to
be a fraud? It would not take many changes to rewrite the

book in that way. A few alterations in the introduction, a few others at other key points would do the job. At these junctures, I would step forward and say, This is where a Mormon and non-Mormon historian will part company. Here is what you can learn if you will follow me. Once again, candor is the best policy. Why didn't I see that earlier? Live and learn.

Will I ever have the chance to issue a second edition of the book? Probably not, though Jed desperately wishes I would. He wants the endnote system revised to include the full citations in the notes and thus reduce the bloated list of "Works Cited" in the back. He has a list of other revisions he would make. None of these strike me as nearly as important as my new perspective. Even short of revising the book, however, I can adopt this perspective in my talks to non-Mormons. Begin confessionally and go from there. I need not be embarrassed about my Mormonism; it is a fact of my life. I think it would relieve everyone to get this out on the table. The questions probing my belief yesterday at the Lehman Center discussion revealed the widespread and natural curiosity to know where I stand.

May 3, 2006

An editor at Knopf called today about the paperback edition due for publication in February 2007. She was unusually curious about the reception of the book. I could not quite grasp the drift of her questions, but I think she really wanted to know how Church leaders felt about the biography. I don't know if she was merely curious or testing the waters for future sales. So far, sales have been great—70,000 copies, she said, though I think she meant copies printed. I told her there has been intense interest among Mormons, some of whom were surprised but more were pleased with the book. General Authorities for the most part have praised it. I said doubtless some objected but a negative opinion had not hardened among Church leaders. She asked about my thoughts on the cover. She began as all the editors do by saying she liked the current dust jacket. I told her there was an alternate dust jacket I liked better, and she promised to consider it. A list of errors has already been submitted. That means that for the time being, I have no obligations. The book will get into the works, I will see a new cover design, and perhaps proofs but probably not. They don't want me to consider revisions. At this point, I am quite happy to let the book live its own life, warts and all.

May 21, 2006

I have come and gone twice over the past two weeks. On May 12, I was at Notre Dame for a conference on John Woolman, the Quaker visionary, to mark the installation of Tom Slaughter in a named chair in early American history. I contributed a somewhat rambling discourse on Slaughter's take on Woolman in a forthcoming book, ending with a brief comparison of Woolman and Smith. The next day I gave a 1:00 p.m. fireside to fifty or sixty Latter-day Saints assembled by Patrick Mason, a comrade from the Joseph Smith Seminar days. The following week, *RSR* was the subject of discussion in Nauvoo by a group of evangelical and Mormon scholars that meets a couple of times a year to talk differences and similarities. I can scarcely characterize the discussion, it sped off in so many directions. To my relief the evangelicals spoke as if they benefitted from the book, contrary to my impression that non-Mormon scholars found it all too laudatory and believing. At the Woolman conference the previous week, Susan Juster, one of the panelists, said that, in her review of the book for *Reviews in American History*, she would conclude that a naturalist explanation was called for, the view expressed by Laurie Maffly-Kipp in *Books and Culture*. Did this mean my plea for empathy was going unheeded and that my work was useless for the non-Mormon reader? The friendly comments of the evangelicals, offered to be sure in a face-to-face meeting that required at least polite approval, was evidence on the other side.

The most telling question came from Richard Mouw, president of Fuller Theological Seminary and one of the guiding lights of these ongoing discussions. "What am I to make of Joseph Smith?" he wanted to know. I offered this and that while he looked back rather uncomprehendingly. The trouble is that I don't know his categories. What boxes does he have in mind for locating Joseph? Unfortunately, Latter-day Saint scholars have not been particularly helpful to Mouw. We are so intent on making Joseph out as a true prophet, we have little to say to Mouw-like readers. A genius and maverick certainly, but where else does he fit? I am thinking gnostic right now since Joseph produced the books of Moses and Abraham that so closely resemble the pseudigraphic works of the four centuries around Christ's life. I made a plea for him to tolerate discursive explorations of Christian doctrine as positive indicators of religious vitality.

May 31, 2006

We returned from Casper, Wyoming, on Monday afternoon. For many months I have been looking forward to the Mormon History Association meetings held there this year to honor the handcart companies. One of the highlights of the program was a performance of "1856: Long Walk Home," a concert opera composed by our daughter-in-law Harriet Bushman. The MHA performance was the last in a series that included the Assembly Hall in Salt Lake City, BYU, and the Provo and Logan tabernacles. It was a moving and powerful show that elicited standing ovations at every performance.

My own long-anticipated encounter with the critics came at the end of a panel discussion on *Rough Stone Rolling* with

Bill Russell, the acerbic and witty Graceland University professor; Dan Vogel, author of *Joseph Smith: The Making of a Prophet* and perhaps Joseph's chief antagonist these days; Gary Topping, a Catholic faculty member at Salt Lake Community College; and Martha Sonntag Bradley-Evans, University of Utah faculty member and author of the Nauvoo volume in the forthcoming Signature Books trilogy on Joseph Smith. Weeks ago as the session was being organized, I had objected to Newell Bringhurst that no one on the panel represented the typical reader in the MHA audience who is likely to be a believing Latter-day Saint. Only Martha Bradley comes close. Bill Russell did his usual witty thing with lots of wisecracks and a scattering of zingers about problems passed over in the book. Gary Topping turned out to be the most polemical participant with a passionate insistence that I had no right to express my faith in Joseph until I had confronted every problem in the Joseph Smith story, none of which to my recollection he specifically mentioned. Dan was gracious and dignified, spotting the key passages where I express my believing perspective. He took issue, but gently and reasonably. Martha dropped her criticism of my plural marriage chapters from her comment, probably to balance the session, and devoted herself to praising the virtues of the book.

Listening to these scholars for about an hour, I decided to view them all as part of a wider Mormon culture. As I said at the outset of my remarks, all of them are attached to Mormonism in some compelling way: Bill Russell has to deal with a host of irksome points in the story; Topping was obviously passionate about the force of the evidence showing Joseph to be a fraud; Dan has devoted himself more completely to Joseph Smith than anyone living, with his long string of scholarly books; Martha showed her affection for Joseph Smith in every word of her comment. While Mormons may think of Sunday School and home teaching as Mormon culture, the work of these four is also part of the Mormon whole. The intensity of their interest helps us to recognize the flaws in our conventional divisions into faithful and unfaithful, believing and unbelieving, active and inactive. We all attach ourselves to Mormonism in some peculiar fashion; we all have our irksome points where we don't feel comfortable and particular sites where we obtain a purchase on our religion. We should recognize that we all are part of big-tent Mormonism and acknowledge each other as brothers and sisters.

My purpose in writing the book, I told this audience, was to present all of Joseph Smith as far as I could grasp him. I worry about the young Latter-day Saints who learn only about the saintly Joseph and are shocked to discover his failings. The problem is that they may lose faith in the entire teaching system that brought them along. If their teachers covered up Joseph Smith's flaws, what else are they hiding? My aim was to make the whole story of this man part of common knowledge in the Church.

I had hoped that I could persuade general readers, I told the audience, to follow me into the religious world of Joseph Smith, the way I like to follow authors into the religious world of Mohammad or George Fox. To my dismay, even sympathetic readers have said that this will not work. Academic readers, they say, want a naturalistic explanation of Joseph's revelations. These insist that everyone think the way they do or they cannot claim to be thinkers at all. But there are drawbacks to this kind of severe rationalism. In practice it ends up stopping inquiry. If you are persuaded that Joseph Smith was a fraud, it is almost impossible to take him seriously. Fawn Brodie found Joseph Smith faintly ridiculous. She was bemused rather than bewitched by him. Nothing he thought or did could be taken entirely seriously because it was all part of his game.

If I were to write again, I told the crowd, I would probably emphasize my belief more than I did. I would say to readers that I can show you a Joseph Smith that a non-believer will probably never see. The fact is that you have to believe in a text in order to take it seriously. Only a lover of Shakespeare is likely to see all there is in his plays. When writing about Hamlet, a critic has to suspend disbelief in the fictionality of the drama and treat it as a portrait of real life; otherwise he will never recover all the currents running through the story. Historically, the close reading of literary texts grew out of believers' close reading of the Bible; it was in reading scripture that readers learned to parse every word in the belief that treasures would be revealed. We read literature closely because it has replaced the Bible as the source of wisdom. No one is likely to treat the Book of Mormon with that regard except believers—or those who suspend disbelief and take the text seriously. We the Mormons should be the ones to scrutinize Joseph Smith's texts in search of treasures.

I cannot remember exactly how I wound up the talk but somehow I came out with a sentence referring to the melee that is Mormon culture. As I sat down, a few people in the audience stood up applauding. Martha told me to take a bow, which I did. I certainly came away from the conference with enough plaudits to buffer the panel's criticism. I now know pretty much what to expect at these events. I know I have the educated Mormons with me; I also have the respect of most non-Mormon scholars but not their acquiescence. I have not given them a Joseph they can believe in. Jan Shipps called this morning to say that she was going to ask either Jon Butler or Skip Stout to contribute to a panel on the book at the American Society of Church Historians next January. She hopes also to persuade Laurel Ulrich to participate. Laurel, of course, is a defender but she is certain to be critical too, especially of the book's treatment of women. So the toasting and roasting will continue. I do believe I am rising above the fray, buoyed by all the Mormons who have benefited from the book. I am satisfied that I did as well as I could with Joseph Smith.

A Final Word

[In July I wrote the brief essay for the online journal *Common-Place* that Laurel Ulrich asked for earlier in the year. It seems like a good way to wrap up the diary.]

"The Balancing Act"
By Richard Lyman Bushman
Common-Place
August 2006

Most reviews of my recent biography, *Joseph Smith: Rough Stone Rolling*, mention that I am a practicing Mormon. The Sunday *New York Times* titled its review, "Latter-Day [sic] Saint: A practicing Mormon delivers a balanced biography of the church's founder, Joseph Smith." Perhaps a little oversensitive, I wondered why this was news. Was a Mormon telling the story of the Church's founding prophet with a degree of objectivity something like man bites dog? Did the editor mean that a mind capable of embracing Mormonism would surely be incapable of a balanced portrayal? Or that Mormonism evokes loyalties so deep that a dispassionate approach to Joseph Smith required a superhuman effort? One reviewer spoke of walking a high wire between the demands of Church conformity and the necessary openness of scholarly investigation. Another, surprised by the balance of the book but unwilling to trust me entirely, said it achieved a "veneer of credibility."

The nearly universal notice of my religion got me to thinking about passion, commitment, and balance. What is the place of personal values and beliefs in scholarship? Our personal commitments bias our work, but is that necessarily bad? Historians write with passion about slavery, race, women, war and peace, freedom, and injustice. Is their work marred by their belief? Beyond question, their values shape the work. After the civil rights movement, we write differently about women and race than we did a half century ago. Are the biases that play about our scholarship prejudices to be purged, or are they powerful and useful motivations?

An impassioned graduate student once announced in a seminar that she could find traces of gender on a blank wall. Her commitment had sharpened her eye for evidence that less engaged researchers missed. I can remember the time when historians sighed that so little evidence about slaves had survived that their lives, regrettably, could never be recovered. Nowadays one would pause before saying that about any subject. As the Gospels say, those who search, find. Passion may introduce bias but it also produces persistence—and data.

Okay, that may be true, we say, for gender studies or investigations of race, but does it work for Joseph Smith with his angelic visitors, gold plates, and a Urim and Thummim? Isn't that a different kind of commitment that borders on the crazy? How can belief in such oddities be allowed any place in scholarship?

I would be the first to admit that my account of Joseph Smith shows greater tolerance for Smith's remarkable stories than most historians would allow. I write about the visits of angels as if they might have happened. I do not assume, a priori, that Joseph Smith's stories are fraudulent, any more than I would automatically write about Mohammad's visions or the biblical miracles as obvious deceptions. But I hope that my readers see that my writing as a believer is not just a personal indulgence. I would like them to understand the benefit for historical inquiry as a whole in writing out of my convictions. The bizarre nature of Joseph Smith's stories makes historical work by a believing historian all the more useful.

One reason is that skepticism about the gold plates and the visions can easily slip over into cynicism. The assumption that Smith concocted the stories of angels and plates casts a long shadow over his entire life. Everything he did is thrown into doubt. His exhortations to godly service, his self-sacrifice, his pious letters to his wife, his apparent love for his fellow workers all appear as manipulations to perpetuate a grand scheme. Cynicism has its advantages in smoking out hypocrisy but it does not foster sympathetic understanding. Every act is prejudged from the beginning.

My advantage as a practicing Mormon is that I believe enough to take Joseph Smith seriously. If a writer begins with the idea that Smith was a fraud who perpetrated a hoax upon the gullible public with his story of gold plates and ancient Israelites in America, nothing he did can be trusted. Every act, every thought is undercut by his presumed fraudulent beginnings. That overhanging doubt makes it difficult for a skeptical biographer to find much of interest in Smith's writings or to explain why thousands of people believed him. What of value is to be expected from the theological meanderings of a charlatan?

A few empathetic historians like Jan Shipps have written with great insight about early Mormonism, but more often than not, skeptical historians brush Joseph Smith's writings aside as banal or vapid. Fawn Brodie, author of a widely accepted biography of Smith, found his religion faintly ridiculous. Her *No Man Knows My History* summarized his teachings only to dismiss them as derivative or strange. She could not explain why thousands of converts to Mormonism devoted their lives to building a Zion in the Great Basin, or what was so enthralling in Smith's vision of a God who was once a man. A more recent biography, Dan Vogel's *Joseph Smith: The Making of a Prophet*, intensely scrutinizes the Book of Mormon but finds nothing compelling or profound in it. On the whole, disbelief dampens this kind of inquiry, and for good reason. People with little concern for the plight of slaves do not scour the sources for clues to slave lives; and skeptics about Mormonism do not work at penetrating the mind of a pretended prophet. It is less a question of intellectual perspicuity than of motivation.

Passion and belief are certainly not requirements for historical inquiry, but neither are they crippling handicaps. Once we relinquish, as we must, the "noble dream" of objective history, personal commitment becomes a valuable resource. We continually develop new readings of Reconstruction or Andrew Jackson because our personal viewpoints based on our values enable us to discover new perspectives. Contrary to the idea that belief closes the mind, our passions open our eyes and ears. Stifling my belief in Joseph Smith would extinguish one of my greatest assets.

Passion, of course, can blind as well as enliven us. There is a danger of descending into undisciplined subjectivity. My belief could produce a Joseph Smith that only the Mormons would recognize. Mormon writers have produced plenty of hagiographies. But there is a check on unbalanced writing—the audience. If I write for Mormons alone, I can indeed create an idealized Prophet worthy of founding a new religion, and many Mormon readers will raise no objections. By the same token, if one writes exclusively for a non-Mormon audience, Joseph Smith can be made into a rogue without fear of contradiction. No one will say, "Not so fast." The reason Mormons disliked Fawn Brodie's biography of Joseph Smith was that she had no regard for Mormon readers. Mormons thought she caricatured Smith, minimizing his religious feelings and downplaying his theological ingenuity. But she did not care; she had written the book for another audience.

As I set out to write *Rough Stone Rolling*, I tried to keep all kinds of readers with me. I vowed not to make Brodie's mistake of writing solely for one part of the potential audience. She wrote for unbelievers; I did not want to err in the opposite direction. My historical instincts moved me to tell the story truthfully anyway, but I also knew that if I overly idealized Smith, I would lose credibility with non-Mormons. With a broad readership in mind, I could not conceal his flaws. Moreover, I tried to voice unbelieving readers' likely reactions when Smith married additional wives or taught doctrines foreign to modern sensibilities. When he went beyond the pale, I acknowledged readers' dismay.

Even though I wrote for a diverse audience, as the reviews came in I realized, that I had not kept everyone with me. As was probably inevitable, readers who came to the book with their own strong notions of Smith found my account wanting. Those on the Mormon side thought I failed to describe his noble character and supernatural gifts; non-Mormons said I painted too rosy a picture and failed to acknowledge the obvious fraud. At both ends of the spectrum, I lost readers.

At times I thought there was no middle ground for my version of the Mormon Prophet. I came to envy historians who write about slavery or patriarchy; no one doubts their basic beliefs. But on second thought, I realized that my book was better for being written for a divided audience. I cannot say that *Rough Stone Rolling* achieves a perfect balance, but it does offer an empathetic and, so I hope, a candid view of an extraordinary life.

Richard Lyman Bushman

Index

Note on Type

William Caslon was known in eighteenth-century England as the first important punchcutter (designer of typefaces) in the English language. At that time, Dutch designers were the principal creators of the typefaces that were imported to England. From 1720 until his death in 1766, William Caslon created many typefaces, some of which bear his name, and he became the first highly distinguished English punchcutter. Of his typefaces, his Caslon became his most famous and durable creation. In America, the script of kings—as his Caslon was known—was used for the Declaration of Independence in 1776. It continues to be one of the most admired faces in the world. Caslon's original specimen sheets and punches have been source material for endlessly tweaked and copied fonts into the digital age. This volume is printed in Caslon #3 Roman, an American variant font, which is slightly heavier than the original.

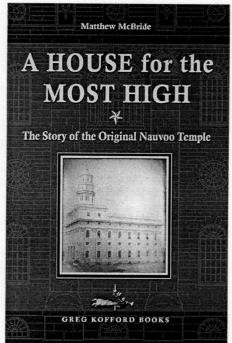

A HOUSE FOR THE MOST HIGH: The Story of the Original Nauvoo Temple
by Matthew McBride

Chronologically documents the behind-the-scenes stories of the common people involved in the sacrifice to erect the second Mormon temple. Firsthand accounts are drawn from diaries, journals, letters, and newspaper articles.

The prologue of this book discusses briefly the early temple building efforts of the fledgling Church of Jesus Christ of Latter-day Saints, the development of temple-related doctrines during the decade prior to the Nauvoo era, and the arrival of the Saints in Illinois in 1839. The body of the history covers the years 1840, when the temple was first contemplated, to 1850, when its walls were toppled by a tornado. An epilogue completes the story by recounting the story of the repurchase of the temple lot by the Church in 1937, the lot's excavation in 1962, and the announcement that the temple would be rebuilt. Also included is an appendix containing important eyewitness descriptions of the temple and a bibliography of major sources.

448 pages

Limited, Signed and Numbered Leather Edition, ISBN 1-58958-021-4
Hardcover, ISBN 1-58958-016-8

MODERN POLYGAMY AND MORMON FUNDAMENTALISM:

The Generations after the Manifesto
by Brian C. Hales

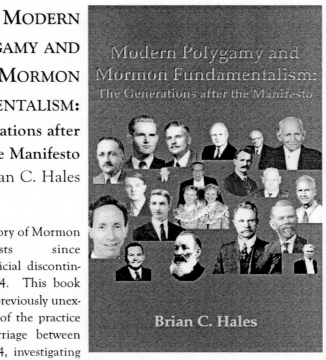

Survey history of Mormon Fundamentalists since polygamy's official discontinuation in 1904. This book examines the previously unexplored period of the practice of plural marriage between 1904 and 1934, investigating the assertion that many plural marriages were solemnized under claims of a new priesthood line of authority asserted by Lorin Woolley. It also focuses on modern-day polygamists many of whom accepted Woolley's teachings and authority, creating many of the fundamentalist organizations during those years after the Manifesto. The Allreds, the FLDS Church on the Utah-Arizona border and in Texas, the Kingstons, the LeBarons, the TLC Church in Manti, Utah, and other splinter groups are all scrutinized in this study. Regardless of one's beliefs regarding Joseph Smith and plural marriage, this historical and doctrinal volume will provide interesting reading and enlightenment.

530 pages

Hardback, ISBN:1-58958-035-4

THE WASP

A newspaper published in Nauvoo from April 16, 1842 through April 26, 1843, *The Wasp* provides a crucial window into firsthand accounts of the happenings and concerns of the Saints in Nauvoo. It was initially edited by William Smith, younger brother of Joseph Smith. William was succeeded by John Taylor as editor and Taylor and Wilford Woodruff as printers and publishers. Some of the main stories that are covered in the newspaper are the August 1842 elections where local candidates endorsed by the Mormons easily won their elections, the fall from grace of John C. Bennett, the attempt by the state of Missouri to extradite Joseph Smith as an accessory in the attempted murder of Lilburn W. Boggs, and the Illinois legislature's effort to repeal the Nauvoo charter.

With foreword by Peter Crawley, putting the newspaper into historical context, this first ever reproduction of the entire run of the *The Wasp* is essential to anyone interested in the Nauvoo period of Mormonism.

216 pages, Oversized 17" X 11"

Limited Edition, 3/4 Leather with hand-marbled boards, 120 numbered copies, ISBN 1-58958-049-4
Hardcover, ISBN 1-58958-050-8

APOCRYPHAL WRITINGS and the Latter-day Saints

This classic volume of essays takes an in-depth look at the Apocrypha and how Latter-day Saints should approach them in their gospel study. With notable LDS authors such as Stephen E. Robinson, Joseph F. McConkie, and Robert L. Millet this volume is an essential addition to any well rounded Mormon studies library. Essays include: "Whose Apocrypha? Viewing Ancient

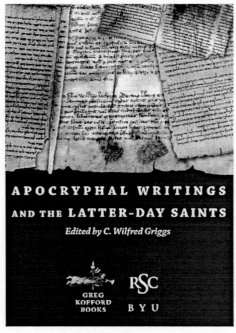

APOCRYPHAL WRITINGS
AND THE LATTER-DAY SAINTS
Edited by C. Wilfred Griggs

GREG KOFFORD BOOKS

RSC BYU

Apocrypha from the Vantage of Events in the Present Dispensation," "Lying for God: The Uses of Apocrypha" and "The Nag Hammadi Library: A Mormon Perspective."

Edited by C. Wilfred Griggs

Religious Studies Center - Brigham Young University

333 pages

Limited, Signed and Numbered Leather Edition, ISBN 1-58958-088-5

Paper, ISBN 1-58958-089-3

MORMONISM AND EVOLUTION: The Authoritative LDS Statements

MORMONISM
AND EVOLUTION:
THE AUTHORITATIVE
LDS STATEMENTS

William E. Evenson & Duane E. Jeffery

The Church of Jesus Christ of Latter-day Saints (the Mormon Church) has generally been viewed by the public as anti-evolutionary in its doctrine and teachings. But official statements on the subject by the Church's highest governing quorum and/or President have been considerably more open and diverse than is popularly believed.

This book compiles in full all known authoritative statements (either authored or formally approved for publication) by the Church's highest leaders on the topics of evolution and the origin of human beings. The authors provide historical context for these statements that allows the reader to see what stimulated the issuing of each particular document and how they stand in relation to one another.

William Evenson is a physics professor at UVSC. Previously, his 34-year tenure at BYU included Dean of Physical and Mathematical Sciences.

Duane E. Jeffery is Professor of Integrative Biology at Brigham Young University.

120 pages

Limited, Signed and Numbered Leather Edition, ISBN 1-58958-097-4
Paper, ISBN 1-58958-092-3

Exploring Mormon Thought, Vol. 2: The Problems of Theism
by Blake T. Ostler

In volume 2 of the three volume series, *Exploring Mormon Thoght, The Problems of Theism and the Love of God*, Blake Ostler explores issues related to soteriology, or the theory of salvation. He argues that the commitment that God loves us and respects our dignity as persons entails that God must leave us free to choose whether to have a saving relationship with him. He explores the "logic of love" and argues that the LDS doctrine of a "war in heaven" embodies the commitment that God leaves us free to choose whether to enter into relationship with God. He explores the nature of inter-personal prayer and the contributions of LDS beliefs to a robust prayer dialogue. He offers a view consistent with LDS commitments that makes sense out of asking God to assist others, to alter the natural environment and to grow in relationship with God.

Praise for the *Exploring Mormon Thought* series:

"These books are the most important works on Mormon theology ever written. There is nothing currently available that is even close to the rigor and sophistication of these volumes. B. H. Roberts and John A. Widtsoe may have had interesting insights in the early part of the twentieth century, but they had neither the temperament nor the training to give a rigorous defense of their views in dialogue with a wider stream of Christian theology. Sterling McMurrin and Truman Madsen had the capacity to engage Mormon theology at this level, but neither one did."   ~Richard Sherlock, *FARMS Review*

480 pages
Vol. 2, Hardback, ISBN 1-58958-095-8
Vol. 1, Hardback, ISBN 1-58958-003-6

HUGH NIBLEY: A CONSECRATED LIFE

The Authorized Biography by Boyd Jay Petersen

As one of the LDS Church's most widely recognized scholars, Hugh Nibley is both an icon and an enigma. Through complete access to Nibley's correspondence, journals, notes and papers, Petersen has painted a portrait that reveals the man behind the legend.

Starting with a foreword written by Zina Nibley Petersen (the author's wife and Nibley's daughter) and finishing with appendixes that include some of the best of Nibley's personal correspondence, the biography reveals aspects of the tapestry of the life of one who has truly consecrated his life to the service of the Lord.

Winner of the Mormon History Association's Best Biography Award.

" . . . this authorized biography is delightfully accessible and full of the scholar's delicious wordplay and wit . . . "

~Publishers Weekly

"Well written and thoroughly researched, Petersen's biography is a must-have for anyone struggling to reconcile faith and reason."

~ Greg Taggart, Association for Mormon Letters

447 pages

Hardback, ISBN 1-58958-020-6
Signed, Numbered Limited Leather, ISBN 1-58958-019-2

PENNY TRACTS AND POLEMICS: A Critical Analysis of Anti-Mormon Pamphleteering in Great Britain, 1837-1860
by Craig L. Foster

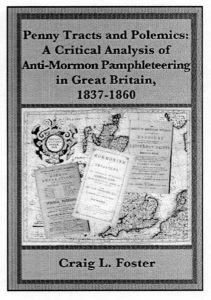

By 1860, Mormonism had enjoyed a presence in Great Britain for over twenty years. Mormon missionaries experienced unprecedented success in conversions and many new converts had left Britain's shores for a new life and a new religion in the far western mountains of the American continent.

With the success of the Mormons came tales of duplicity, priestcraft, sexual seduction and uninhibited depravity among the new religious adherents. Thousands of pamphlets were sold or given to the British populace as a way of discouraging people from joining the Mormon Church. Foster places the creation of these English anti-Mormon pamphlets in their historical context. He discusses the authors, the impact of the publications and the Mormon response. With illustrations and detailed bibliography.

260 pages

Hardback, ISBN 1-58958-005-2
Signed, Numbered Limited Leather, ISBN 1-58958-044

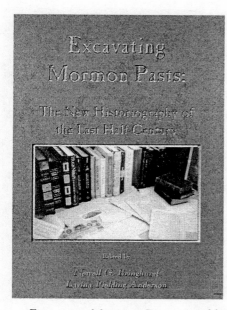

EXCAVATING MORMON PASTS:

The New Historiography of the Last Half Century

Edited by Newell Bringhurst and Lavina Fielding Anderson

Includes Mormon History Association Award Winning Essay by Roger Launius

Excavating Mormon Pasts assembles sixteen knowledgeable scholars from both LDS and the Com-munity of Christ traditions who have long participated skillfully in this dialogue. It presents their insightful and sometimes incisive surveys of where the New Mormon History has come from and which fields remain unexplored. Both a vital reference work and a stimulating picture of the New Mormon History in the early twenty-first century.

Winner of the Special Book Award from the John Whitmer Historical Association

"[*Excavating Mormon Pasts* is] a valuable tool in the ongoing quest for clarity, for truth, for certainty. It is one of several volumes I've seen in the past few years that qualify for a 'must have' rating."

~ Jeffrey Needle, Association for Mormon Letters

442 pages

Hardback, ISBN 1-58958-091-5
Signed, Numbered Limited Leather, ISBN 1-58958-090-7

THE INCOMPARABLE
JESUS
by Grant H. Palmer

Distilled from his personal and teaching experiences, this tender testament to the incomparable Jesus describes a Savior who walked the halls with him, succoring those in need.

In this slim volume, Palmer sensitively shares his understanding of what it means to know Jesus by doing his works. He lists the qualities of divine character attested to by the Apostles Peter and Paul, and also those that Jesus revealed about himself in his masterful Sermon on the Mount, particularly in the beatitudes.

With reverence Palmer shares personal spiritual experiences that were life-changing assurances of Jesus's love for him--a love poured out unstintingly in equally life-changing blessings on prisoners whose crimes have not stopped short of sexual abuse and murder. Reading this book offers deeper understanding of the Savior's mercy, a stronger sense of his love, and a deeper commitment to follow him.

Grant Palmer closed his thirty-four-year career teaching for the LDS Church Educational System with the final thirteen years as a chaplain and the LDS Institute director at the Salt Lake County Jail.

157 pages

Paper, ISBN 1-58958-092-3